THE OWL
IN ART, MYTH, AND LEGEND

Augsburg gilt model of an owl, c. 1630.
The branch at the base forms a whistle.
Such ornaments were kept on the table
and used to summon servants.

THE OWL
IN ART, MYTH, AND LEGEND

Compiled by **Krystyna Weinstein**

'I rejoice that there are owls.'
(Henry David Thoreau)

CRESCENT BOOKS
NEW YORK

Produced by Savitri Books Ltd
Southbank House
Suite 106, Black Prince Road
London SE1 7SJ

This 1989 edition
published by Crescent Books,
distributed by Crown Publishers, Inc.
225 Park Avenue South
New York, New York 10003

ISBN 0-517-68475-6

h g f e d c b a

Designed by Mrinalini Srivastava
Edited by Ailsa Hudson
Picture research by Krystyna Weinstein
Black and white photography by Salim Hafejee and Colin Turner

Printed and bound in Hong Kong

**To Pushkin
An owl–like tabby**

Owl symbol by Terry Reed

HORNED OWL.
Strix Virginiana.

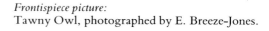

Frontispiece picture:
Tawny Owl, photographed by E. Breeze-Jones.

INTRODUCTION

Campanian black-glazed pottery kylix (drinking vessel), c.3rd century BC.

Throughout the ages and across cultures, the owl has exercised a strange fascination over people. Few other birds or animals have gathered so many different and contradictory beliefs about them: owls have been both feared and venerated, despised and admired, considered wise and foolish, associated with witchcraft and medicine, the weather, births, deaths – and have even found their way into *haute cuisine*.

Literary allusions to the owl begin in earliest folklore, impossible to date, but passed down by word of mouth over generations. In ancient Indian folklore (the antecedent of many of our moral fables, retold much later by La Fontaine), the owl represents wisdom and helpfulness, and has powers of prophecy. This theme recurs in Aesop's fables and in Greek myths and beliefs. As the symbol of Athene, goddess and patron of Athens, the owl was a protector, accompanying Greek armies to war, and providing ornamental inspiration for their daily lives.

Both Aristotle and later Pliny made detailed studies of the world of animals and birds around them, and their observations served as the basis for similar studies during the next few centuries.

By the Middle Ages in Europe, the owl had become the associate of witches and the inhabitant of lonely and profane places, a foolish yet feared apparition. Its wail filled people with foreboding and apprehension: a death was imminent, evil was at hand. The owl's appearance at night, when people could not see, linked it with mischief and the unknown.

The eighteenth century saw a renewed interest in the zoological aspects of owls, and both descriptions and illustrations – from close observation – were detailed. With the dying out of superstitions by the twentieth century – in the West at least – the owl has returned to its position as a symbol of wisdom. Nevertheless, old folktales still tell of an owl's cry portending death in England, the loss of virginity in Wales, and the birth of a daughter in France.

In North America, the medicine men of many Indian peoples venerated the owl, and it was endowed with qualities sought by people in their everyday lives – bravery, clear vision and hunting prowess. Among some Australian Aborigine tribes, women saw the owl as their spiritual guide, and in parts of Asia too, the owl was considered a protector, a divine ancestor, who helped to ward off evil spirits, famine and pestilence.

Simultaneously with its portrayal in literature, the owl made frequent appearances in art. Prehistoric peoples as far apart as France and Australia sketched owls in their caves, and one of the earliest known representations of owls is on a Babylonian statue of Lilith, goddess of death. The owl also appeared on Egyptian tombs as a decoration and as the pictorial symbol of the letter 'm'.

Thereafter, the owl appears in numerous forms in Greek art – particularly in Athenian art – and in Roman art and artefacts. Throughout the Middle Ages, the owl represented the Jews – who were said to live in spiritual darkness, shunned and feared by Christians. The owl was frequently portrayed being mobbed by other birds – a 'natural' justification for the persecutions the Jews were made to endure? In both Europe and other cultures (notably India and Persia) owls appeared in illustrations of texts, both secular and religious. The owl is represented in early woodcuts with witches, demons and other inhabitants of darkness, but also in scenes of the Nativity and the Ark.

With the flowering of art in the Renaissance and the following centuries, the owl continued as a source of inspiration, appearing in sculpture (wood, stone, metal and glass), in textiles, in everyday artefacts (jugs, tiles, goblets), and in paintings and illustrations, from Michelangelo, Dürer and Bosch, to Picasso.

In other cultures, the owl has also appeared on artefacts such as Peruvian Moche pottery jugs, North American Indian pipes and shields, on African masks, and in delicate Chinese and Japanese paintings. In the twentieth century the owl has been used as the logo of learned associations and by book publishers; it is used to advertise products – from reading glasses to computers – or simply as a form of decoration in our homes. The illustrations contained in this book attempt to show the diversity of media for which the owl has provided inspiration.

Detail of illuminated page in a thirteenth-century northern French Bible.

Roman mosaic from the House of Orpheus, Volubilis, Morocco, c.3rd century AD.

Owls ~ Owls

The owl is rather a special bird. As its haunting cry echoes across silent fields, or startles us in tangled woods, and we catch a glimpse of it – an apparition drifting momentarily into sight and then gone – we stop and listen, almost instinctively, and assign some meaning to its presence, more so than to any other bird: it brings good or bad luck, it represents wisdom or folly, it foretells fine or foul weather ... and it retains its mystery, for all the zoological data amassed about it.

The owl has also provided us with a vast verbal imagery: a drunk is described as owl-eyed, an owlglass is a jester, and mere stupidity is owlish. Night-lovers are, inevitably, owls, who spend their time owlin' round, even if their night roving is with innocent intentions, and the New York Third Avenue all-night trains of the late nineteenth century were known as owl trains. Owl-light precedes the owl's unnatural night-time activities, when it cavorts with witches and spirits, mingling deadly potions to owl-blast, or bewitch, some unsuspecting victim.

In error, or wantonly, through fear or for food, or merely in sport, the owl has been persecuted to near extinction in some places: maybe the

Barn Owls by John Busby.

7

Arabs are correct in believing that the cry of an owl is a curse in its own language.

In most languages the word for 'owl' is onomatopoeic: (Italian) *guffo*, *civetta*; (French) *hibou*, *chouette*; (Polish) *sowa*; (German) *Eule, Uhu*; (Latin) *bubo*; (Danish) *ugle*; (Japanese) *fukuro*, *mimizuku*; (Chinese) *chixiu*; (Hindi) *ulu*.

The Chinese also sometimes call the owl: *maoton ying* – cat-headed bird.

Human fascination with owls seems to be endless and timeless. There are prehistoric rock drawings of owls in places as far apart as France and Australia. Were they drawn purely as decoration, or did they have some other significance? It is impossible to know. It is certain, however, that many old legends, beliefs and everyday tales, originally handed down orally by the light of the fire, were modified as they moved across continents and down through time, but they all expressed people's mixed feelings about this strange – some might say unnatural – bird. Unnatural because its appearance and behaviour sets it apart from other birds: it comes to life at night, it sees in the dark, its song is unlike that of any other bird and its head and face bear an uncanny resemblance to those of a cat. 'Feathered wild cat' was in fact the verdict of W.H. Hudson, the early twentieth-century English writer and naturalist. A contemporary was also struck by the owl's appearance: 'It is only a cat on wings [whose] conversation is a trifle disconcerting to nervous folk.'

Edward Lear, the nineteenth-century English writer and painter, must have also noticed this resemblance, for he sent these two unlikely companions in search of happiness:

The Owl and the Pussy-cat went to sea
In a beautiful pea-green boat:
They took some honey, and plenty of money
Wrapped up in a five-pound note.
The Owl looked up to the stars above,
And sang to a small guitar,
'O lovely Pussy, O Pussy, my love,
What a beautiful Pussy you are,
You are,
You are!
What a beautiful Pussy you are!'
(Edward Lear, *The Owl and the Pussy-cat*, 1889)

A slightly less amiable encounter between these cousins was observed in Georgia by Thomas Nuttall, the nineteenth-century American naturalist:

8

'Prowling around his premises, the owl saw a cat dozing on the roof of
the smoke-house, and supposing Grimalkin a more harmless rabbit-like
animal than appeared in the sequel, blindly snatched her up in his
talons; but finding he had caught a Tartar, it was not long before he
allowed Puss once more to tread the ground ...'
(Thomas Nuttall, *Manual of Ornithology of the
United States and Canada*, 1832–34)

The strange and haunting song of the owl has long given rise to comment and speculation. A Spanish legend tells how the owl used to sing
sweetly, but its presence at Christ's crucifixion meant that ever after-
wards it could only repeat the words *cruz, cruz* (cross, cross). An old
Hawaiian war chant spoke of *ka pueo kani kava* (the owl who sings),
and Pliny, the Roman writer, scholar and naturalist, reported in the first
century AD that 'the owl sings in nine different notes'.

In a letter to a fellow naturalist, Thomas Pennant, the Rev. Gilbert
White, writing from his peaceful parish of Selbourne in Hampshire, was
intrigued by the owl's musical achievements:

'A neighbour of mine who is said to have a nice ear, remarks that the

owls about this village hoot in three different keys, in G flat, or F sharp, in B flat and A flat. He hears two hooting to each other, the one in A flat, the other in B flat. Query: do these different notes proceed from different species, or only from various individuals?'
(Rev. Gilbert White, *The Natural History of Selbourne*, 1789)

Detail from the *Survey of Glastonbury Abbey Property*, c.1539.

Washington Irving's owl, however, who befriended the young and unworldly Prince Ahmed and helped him to overcome the problems posed by love to which the singing birds of springtime had introduced him, had no pretensions to musical talent: 'These singing birds ... I despise them and their themes. Allah be praised I cannot sing.' (*Tales of*

Small sconce in the shape of an owl.

the Alhambra, 1832). One wonders what he would have thought of the barking owl encountered by a traveller to Oporto in Portugal: 'It lived near the door on an ordinary parrot perch ... It became very excited when it saw any small dog, and imitated a bark to attract it.'

An owl hoot is quite an easy sound for people to imitate: by cupping the hands together and blowing through them, the noise produced does resemble the hoot of an owl. In Illinois it was regarded as unlucky to do this, but the American adventurer, Davy Crockett, in his *Almanack* for 1835, told his gullible readers that hunters in the West used to imitate the cry of the Barred Owl when out hunting the wild turkey, for that bird would invariably gobble back each time, thereby disclosing its whereabouts.

Some claim that Robin Hood and his Merrie Men signalled to each other in Sherwood Forest by hooting like owls, thereby confusing the Sheriff of Nottingham. Another group, the Chouans, who smuggled contraband salt during the chaotic years that followed the French Revolution and who claimed to be Royalists, are known definitely to have contacted each other during their nightly activities by using the cry of the owl – hence their name, from the Breton word *chouan*, meaning Screech Owl.

The mysterious nightly antics of the owl gradually became part of popular imagery and were used to describe a variety of human nefarious activities. Phrases like 'flying by owl-light' and 'to fly with the owl' became synonymous with breaking the law after dark in seventeenth-century England, and 'owling' was the night-time smuggling of wool and sheep from Kent and Sussex to the ports of northern France. In recognition of this illicit activity the French even had a saying *larron comme une chouette* – to thieve like an owl.

The owl has also played a part in the warring traditions of different regions of the world. It is said that Agathocles, the tyrant of Syracuse, ordered a number of owls to be released among his troops before attacking the Carthaginians; the birds flew through the column and settled on the soldiers' shields and helmets. This boosted the morale of the soldiers who took it as a favourable omen because the owl was sacred to the goddess of war Athene.

Pliny also noted the power of the owl's presence in battle: '... whosoever carry about them the heart [of an owl] when they go to fight shall become more hardy, and perform their work the better against their enemies.' (*Natural History*, 1st century AD).

In the folklore of the American Indians too, the owl seems to have taken an active part in warfare. It is said that the Pima Indian chief urged his men against the Apaches and called upon the owl for assistance:

'. . . [the owl] looked about and saw my plan . . . He cut the power of the enemy, their springs, their trees, their dreams. He grasped their bows and arrows, and bit them in twain. He bit off their flesh and sinews, and made holes in their bones . . .'

(Frank Russell, The Pima Indians, 1908)

The Tlingi Indian warriors of North America had similar faith in the owl; they would rush into battle on a surge of adrenalin, hooting like owls – presumably to give themselves confidence and to put the fear of god into their enemies.

American Indian shield used in Ghost Dance, decorated with painted owl on muslin (Sioux, South Dakota).

The owl has not only caught the imagination of those joined in battle; its slow, rhythmic flight low across the fields at dusk – 'a spectral and unearthly appearance' – has long inspired the poets. George Meredith wrote:

> Lovely are the wings of the white owl sweeping
> Wavy in the dusk lit by one large star ...
> (George Meredith, *Love in the Valley*, 19th century)

And some decades later, the peacefulness of the owl's flight inspired Osbert Sitwell to write:

> An owl, horned wizard of the night,
> Flaps through the air, so soft and still;
> Moans, as it wings its flight
> Toward the mist-wrapped hill.
> (Osbert Sitwell, *Three Nocturnes*, 20th century)

Polish hand-carved wooden toy in the shape of an owl, from Bialystok.

Man has long had associations of a mystical nature with the owl. It was widely believed by primitive peoples that they shared with, or acquired from, various birds and animals particular traits and characteristics: strength, gentleness or treachery for instance. How certain birds and animals became associated with these attributes is not always entirely clear. The owl's reputation among some North American Indian tribes for courage or strength probably came from its capacity to strike its prey noiselessly and effectively; hunting peoples would have felt an immediate affinity with this creature and tried to emulate its prowess.

The Ainu of northern Japan, who also depended on hunting for their

Owl from the Tomb of Giuliano de Medici in the Medici Chapel in Florence by Michelangelo, 1526–31. The large figure of 'Night' on the tomb is accompanied by the owl – the bird of night – also frequently associated with death.

14

Below. 'A picture is a poem without words.'

livelihood, used to drink a 'toast' to the Eagle Owl – whom they considered to be a divine ancestor – before setting out on a hunting expedition.

In many cultures the owl came to be regarded as the symbol of wisdom, capable even of foretelling the future. According to a Navaho Indian legend, the creator, Nayenezgani, told the owl upon creating it '... in days to come men will listen to your voice to know what will be their future.' It seems likely that the owl is frequently credited with wisdom because of its solemn appearance and because it is usually observed, particularly by day, motionless, with eyes half-closed as if in contemplation, unaffected by what is going on around it. In the words of the old rhyme:

> A wise old owl sat in an oak
> And the more he sat, the less he spoke,
> And the less he spoke, the more he heard,
> Why can't we all be like that wise old bird.

Symbolising wisdom, owl images are now often found adorning the gates of universities, libraries and other seats of learning.

Among the Aborigines of Australia, owls and women (bats and men) established a kind of kinship, as J.G. Frazer observed in *The Golden Bough*:

'... Among some tribes of Victoria "the common bat belongs to the men who protect it against injury, even to half-killing their wives for its sake. The fern-owl or large goat sucker belongs to the women and although the bird of evil omen, creating terror at night by its cry, it is jealously protected by them. If a man kills one, they are as enraged as if it was one of their children, and will strike him with their long poles." The jealous protection thus afforded by Australian men and women to bats and owls respectively ... is not based purely on selfish considerations ... Each woman believes that the lives of her mother, sister, daughters and so forth, equally her own, are bound up with the lives of particular owls, and that in guarding the owl species, she is guarding the lives of her female relations ...'

(J.G. Frazer, *The Golden Bough*, 1922)

15

By a strange coincidence, in parts of the Indian sub-continent people believed that the owl was in fact married to the bat. The Kwakiutl Indians of North America were convinced that owls were the souls of people and should therefore not be harmed, for when an owl was killed the person to whom the soul belonged would also die.

The Lenape Indians believed that if they dreamt of an owl it would become their guardian, whereas in a somewhat different dream interpretation Artemidorus, the second-century Roman soothsayer, warned that to dream of an owl meant that a traveller would be shipwrecked or robbed. An even worse fate awaited an Apache Indian, to whom dreaming of an owl signified approaching death.

On their remote Pacific atolls, the people of Samoa believed that they were descended from an owl, although it is not known which particular species of owl their ancestor was supposed to have been. The Newuk Indians of California, however, were more specific and believed that, after death, the virtuous and the brave among them became Great Horned Owls, whereas the wicked were doomed to become Barn Owls. It is difficult to know why the helpful Barn Owls were disparaged in this way, but the inhabitants of Tangier also singled them out for harsh judgement, considering them to be the clairvoyants of the devil.

A hand-carved figure from Samoa.

16

The owl has been associated with evil in many traditions, and there are numerous tales of wicked people being changed into owls, as in the Greek legend of Persephone. She was transported to the underworld against her will by Pluto, and was to be allowed to return to her mother, Ceres, provided she ate nothing while in the underworld. Ascalpus, however, saw her picking a pomegranate, told what he had seen, and for his trouble was transformed into an owl – 'a sluggish screech owl, a loathsome bird'.

Being turned into an owl as a punishment – whether deserved or not – is a commonly recorded fate. The fourteenth-century Welsh poet, Dafydd ap Gwilym, tells in his poem *The Owl's Pedigree* of a fair maid being changed into an owl for loving the wrong man. And from northern Borneo comes the tale of Puok, the wife of the Supreme Being Kohlong, who also suffered the same fate at the hands of her husband. He became angry when she told people on Earth about their life on the Moon, and about Kohlong's power over all things in man's life – his birth, his fate and his death.

The baker's daughter was similarly punished – this time for meanness. Christ, the Gloucestershire tale relates, stopped by at her father's shop and asked for some bread. The baker's daughter refused to give him the whole loaf and was instantly changed into an owl. '. . . the owl was a baker's daughter' cries Ophelia (William Shakespeare, *Hamlet*).

It is possible that this story travelled to North America with the first settlers, for there is a version of it told in Virginia: an old man stopped on his travels at a log cabin and asked an old woman for something to eat. She was cooking cowpeas and ash cake, but refused to give him any. She allowed the water to boil away so that the peas did not cook, and she burnt the ash cake. As he left, the old man said 'you're an old owl and shall stay so', and the old woman flew into the fireplace and up the chimney.

Chimneys seem to be attractive to owls – as a vantage point, a source of heat? But owls have also been known to fall down chimneys. George Edwards, the eighteenth-century English artist and naturalist, recalled painting a little owl 'which [had come] down a chimney in St Catherine's parish by the Tower of London.'

An Iroquois Indian legend tells of a small boy whose grandmother went into the loft every evening but would not let him in. Curious to know the reason why, he crept up there one evening, and found an owl's head. He put it on and suddenly assumed the shape of an owl – but a crazy one. He swooped around houses, pulled up the flowers in people's gardens, and eventually fell into a chimney and down into a fireplace. There he was found, a small boy once again, but still wearing the owl's head. He told people what had happened, and this was how it was discovered that his grandmother was a witch!

Flying obviously has its hazards: Pliny observed how the Horned Owl '... cannot fly whither it wishes, in a straight line, but is always carried along by a sideways movement.' (*Natural History*, 1st century AD). Because of their ability to fly – to appear seemingly from nowhere and disappear swiftly into the distant sky, like flights of fancy – birds have always been linked in people's minds with souls or angels, or other supernatural beings: '... a god worshipped in Livonia ... is said to have flown in the shape of an owl to the island of Oesel when Christian soldiers appeared in his temple.' (Charles de Kay, *Bird Gods of Ancient Europe*, 1898).

According to some Sierra tribes of California, the Great Horned Owl captured the souls of the dead and carried them to the other world. In many European countries, people who claim to be completely free of superstition often mention the appearance of owls soon after the death of a loved one. Seeing the owl is frequently accompanied by a deep sense of peace and some inner conviction that the owl is the dead person, or the dead person's soul. In the Arab world it was believed that owls were the souls of people who had been killed, but who were still waiting for their deaths to be avenged. In Romania, on the other hand, the souls of repentant sinners flew to heaven in the guise of White Owls. To the Mojave Indians of Arizona, however, becoming an owl was merely an interim stage after death before becoming a water beetle and, ultimately, pure air.

As airborne creatures, birds have always symbolised freedom and release, and they possess what to us is a skill we have long sought to emulate. This ability to wing their way across the skies marked birds out as carriers of news, good or bad, and owls were frequently regarded as 'death's dreadful messengers' (Spencer). In Indian mythology both the owl and the pigeon were the messengers of Yama, the god of the dead. In Mexico the Little Owl was called 'the messenger of the lord of the land of the dead' and spent its time flying between the two worlds of the

Page 20. Two Snowy Owls by John James Audubon from *The Birds of America*, 1827–38, said to be his only night-time picture. Audubon observed the birds from a pile of drift logs on the Ohio River.

Page 21. Illuminated page from a sixteenth-century Flemish Book of Hours. The text is a penitential psalm and the owl in the border is probably a symbol of doom.

19

Aluco Minor   *Lucheran*   *The White Owl*

Opposite. Common Barn Owl, hand-coloured engraving by Eleazar Albin, *Natural History of Birds*, 1731–38.

living and the dead; in West Africa the owl's function as a messenger was primarily to summon witches and wizards to a cannibal feast or some other hideous gathering.

By and large, the owl is regarded as the bearer of bad news, deserving Chaucer's description of 'the prophete of wo and myschaunce', although on rare occasions it is recounted that the owl brought life-sustaining news. According to an Achomawi Indian legend from northern California, after the Flood, when all the fires in the world had gone out, the owl set out for Mount Shasta to look out over the world to see if he could find any trace of fire. He was gone for a long time, but upon his

Great Horned Owl by George Edwards, *Natural History of Uncommon Birds*, 1743–51. The artist saw this bird in the park of the Earl of Burlington, at his house in Chiswick, near London. The bird had been brought from Virginia.

return said that he had seen smoke in the west coming from a sweat-house where people were taking steam baths. The next day everyone set out west, each carrying a piece of cedar bark with which they brought back fire to their homes. In a Penobscot Indian tale from Maine, the Snowy Owl was sent out from his village in search of water, and after many encounters and adventures he returned home, successful, and was crowned chief of his village.

Good or evil, stupid or wise? Our opinion of the owl seems not to interest it at all. Unruffled by all this unsolicited attention it stares down at us from some vantage point, prompting the twentieth-century American writer William Service's son to comment thus upon an owl seen from an odd perspective: 'Why the owl . . . he looks almost like a bird.' Inevitably the writer is as intrigued as his son by their unusual pet:

'. . . the owl motif these days, in advertising, decorating, cartoons and so forth . . . well, I was going to say, has become a fad, but any image which has recurred through well over two thousand years to look out at us from coin, fresco or necktie deserves a better word than fad. The living owl looks like an exaggeration, an intensification, of what an owl is supposed to look like. He flies and has feathers, so our owl must be a bird, but it takes some self-reminding now and then that Owl *is* a bird.'
(William Service, *Owl*, 1969)

Cartoon by Angus James.

NATURE'S BIRD

Naturalists have been intrigued for centuries by owls, and some of our earliest descriptions come from Greek observers: Alexander of Myndos tells us that the Scops Owl is 'smaller than the little owl, and has whitish spots on its head, coloured plumage, while two feathers sprout from its eyebrows on either side of the temple.' Aristotle noted that the Little Owl 'in disposition is diligent and ingenious', while Pliny observed that '... the birds of the night also have crooked talons ... [and] the sight of all of them is defective.'

In the nineteenth century, Prince Charles Bonaparte, a nephew of the emperor Napoleon, travelled to North America to study its ornithology and observed the fascinating behaviour of the Burrowing Owl, so called because it lives in the burrows of prairie dogs, sometimes even sharing them with the animal. Of this species the prince noted:

'... instead of sailing forth in the obscurity of the evening or morning twilight, and then retreating to mope away the intervening hours ... [it] enjoys the broadest glare of the noon-day sun, and flying rapidly along, searches for food or pleasure during the cheerful light of day.'
(Charles Bonaparte, *American Ornithology*, 1825)

The Burrowing Owl also fascinated the pioneers who travelled across the United States in the nineteenth century. These small, long-legged, round-headed birds watched the passing convoys, always managing to face anyone who approached them. This led to stories that, by circling the owl, it could be made to wring its own neck! In reality, the owl was capable of making such a quick volte-face that the human eye could barely detect it. Sightings of this remarkable bird were also reported in the nineteenth century from Valdivia in Chile: the *Daily News* of June 6, 1896, reported that a Dr Plate had 'observed this remarkable earth owl, which digs long shafts into the steppes, and is distinguished by its terrible screams.'

Etching of a Burrowing Owl.

Early nineteenth-century Indian
Company School watercolour, c.1820.

Young Tawny Owl by R.G. Greenhalf.

The best way of studying a species is, of course, to catch one. A youthful Gerald Durrell, whilst studying animal behaviour on the island of Corfu, one day had his patience rewarded:

'I thrust my arm into a hole and my fingers closed round something small and soft, something that wriggled as I pulled it out. At first glance my capture appeared to be an outsize bundle of dandelion seeds, furnished with a pair of enormous golden eyes; closer inspection proved it to be a young Scops owl, still clad in his baby down. We regarded each other for a moment, and then the bird, apparently indignant at my ill-mannered laughter at his appearance, dug his tiny claws deeply into my thumb, and I lost my grip on the branch, so that we fell out of the tree together.

I carried the indignant owlet home in my pocket, and introduced him to the family with a certain trepidation. To my surprise, he was greeted with unqualified approval, and no objection was raised to my keeping him ...'

(Gerald Durrell, *My Family and Other Animals*, 1956)

The golden eyes mentioned by Gerald Durrell are one of the most striking features of any owl: round, staring, unblinking eyes, with the most amazing night-time vision, able to home in on the smallest prey:

An owl that in a barn
Sees a mouse creeping in the corn,
Sits still and shuts his round blue eyes,
As if he slept, until he spies
The little beast within his reach
Then starts, and seizes on the wretch.
(S. Butler, *Hudibras*, 17th century)

A decidedly short-sighted owl – *Punch* cartoon, 1860.

According to an old French belief, this amazing eyesight also enabled the owl to spot treasures from afar, and it was widely held that, like the magpie, the owl stole and hoarded precious and valuable objects. An old French tale, with a happy ending, tells how such a treasure was found in an owl's nest, high in a castle wall, by a poor peasant who immediately went from rags to riches!

Leonardo da Vinci, in a study on optics in his *Notebooks*, discusses the prodigious night-vision of the owl. He attributes it to the size of the owl's eye being greater than that of its brain, this being particularly true of the Long-eared and Short-eared Owl, the White Owl and the Little Owl, and the Horned Owl. He adds that the diameter of the pupil of the Horned Owl and of the Long-eared Owl at night increases in size by up to ten times the size it is by day.

Scientific evidence aside, to be able to see in the dark – like the owl – is a gift anyone would appreciate. Blindness at night is something we humans find very tedious, and must have found even more so before the advent of electric light. Thus, not surprisingly, from time immemorial numerous concoctions have been prepared from various parts of the owl – all allegedly conferring the gift of night-sight upon those brave enough to drink them. Folk remedies often professed that by eating or making use of a particular bird or animal, human beings could acquire its characteristics. From northern Japan comes this particular recipe:

'Calcine and reduce to powder the feathers of an owl's wing. Dissolve in the juice of ukigusa [a herb] and apply to the eye.'

Bathing a child's eye with water in which an owl's feather had been soaked was the method used by the Cherokees of North America to give the child night-vision, whereas in northern India a more logical method was used: they ate the eyeball of an owl. This rather unpalatable treatment was also used in parts of England, although according to a North African belief it was essential to know which eye to use, for '... one eye of an owl sleeps, but the other is permanently wakeful. In order to tell which is which, the eyes must be put into a bowl of water, when the sleepy eye will sink, while the other floats.' Suspending the sleepy eye, as a charm, over a person suffering from insomnia would, it was said, cure the condition; likewise, suspending the wakeful eye over a sleepy person could be used to keep the latter awake.

Suspicious husbands and fathers in Morocco had a rather different use for the owl's eyes – and one which did not even depend on the cooperation of the wife or daughter. By placing the right eye of an Eagle Owl into the hand of their sleeping wife or daughter they ensured that their womenfolk would tell them exactly what they had been doing during the day. Pliny also reported having heard a similar tale, this time using the heart of a Screech Owl. He was, of course, scornful of such claims:

'I cannot pass over the vanity of magicians which herein appeareth most evidently; for over and besides many other monstrous lies which they have devised, they give out that if one do lay the heart of a scritch owl on the left pap of a woman as she lies asleep, she will disclose and utter all the secrets of her heart ...'

(Pliny, *Natural History*, 1st century AD)

Young Barn Owl by Ralph Thompson.

In heraldry the owl was always represented full-face and symbolised vigilance.

In sixteenth-century England, a superstitious public was also being encouraged to believe in 'the marvellous virtues of this fowl.' Albertus Magnus, in his *Book of Secretes* (1525) wrote:

'... for if the heart and right foot of it be put upon a man sleeping he shall say anon to thee whatsoever thou shalt ask of him.' Moreover, '... if any man puts this [heart] under his armhole, no dog will bark at him, but keep silent.'

The mythology, legends, tales and superstitions surrounding the owl are many. Although sometimes contradictory, they are always fascinating. Whereas some believed that the owl could bestow night-vision or uncover the secrets of the sleeping, others believed the owl to be a lazy bird – a belief founded on its drowsiness and lack of day-time activity. Hence the belief of the Pueblo Indians that an owl feather placed near a wakeful baby would help it to fall asleep.

The belief that an owl is a lazy bird is borne out by the old Breton tale – versions of which are known in other regions of the world. The story goes that the birds of the earth decided to hold a competition – the winner to be crowned king. The eagle and the owl were the main contestants and the bird who could fly the highest would win the crown. Off they both flew, but a small wren had hidden in the eagle's feathers, and when the two bigger birds became exhausted and could go no higher, the wren flew up further and higher into the sky. Upon its return to earth it was crowned king of the birds, but when the deception was discovered the other birds imprisoned the wren, setting the owl to watch over the wren's hole. However, the owl, being a lazy bird, fell asleep, and the wren escaped. This is why, it is said, the owl is now chased and hounded by all the other birds.

Sleepiness, however, is the last thing the Australian Aborigines would accuse the owl of. They have a tale that tells of the conscientious nightwatchman who, even after his death, in the guise of a Little Owl, continued to guard his people and to warn them of approaching danger at night. Many tales are also told by North American Indians of watchful owls who helped them against enemies by granting night-sight to their medicine men.

Page from *The Statutes of England*, late 15th century.

32

To the Teton Sioux the owl was sacred because their medicine men received their powers through dreams as clear as the sight of an owl – and in recognition of this they wore owl feathers.

Among the Pima Indians of the south-western deserts of America, owl feathers were given to the dying – possibly to help them reach the owl who awaited their souls. J.R. Swanton, in a report to the United States Bureau of Ethnology in 1904–5, recounted how the feathers were kept in a long, rectangular box or basket of maguey leaf: 'If the family had no owl feathers at hand they sent to the medicine man who always kept them. If possible the feathers were taken from a live bird . . . the owl might then be set free, or killed.'

As to how the owl came to possess feathers, there is a legend from the North-East Frontier near Afghanistan which tells how man originally had feathers and wings, but no fire. Nearby lived an owl who had both flint and iron and used to light fires with them to keep himself warm, for he was without feathers and felt the cold. One day, man met the owl and in exchange for the flint and iron he gave the owl wings and feathers, thus enabling the owl to fly and man to make fire.

Elf Owl, pen-and-ink drawing by Norman Arlott.

33

Presumably because he knew the disadvantages of being without feathers, the owl cherished them greatly for, according to ancient folklore, after the wren had scorched its feathers after flying too close to the sun in search of fire for the other birds, they all offered it some of their own feathers – all, that is, except the owl. This, so the stories go, is why the owl now lurks all day long in a hole, because the other birds were so angry with it for its selfishness.

The Eagle and the Owl from La Fontaine's *Fables*, illustrated by Gustave Doré, 1867.

Odo of Cheriton, a Kentish preacher of the twelfth century and one of the earliest English fable writers, has a different explanation for the owl hiding its face by day: it had stolen the rose, which was the prize awarded for beauty, and the other birds punished it by allowing it to come out only at night. A rather vain owl in a Polish tale, however, explains that it does not come out by day for its beauty would so bewitch the other birds that it would run the risk of being mobbed by them.

'Beauty in owls is a dangerous possession.' Rev. F.O. Morris.

The owl's claim to beauty is debatable, and on at least one occasion it cost the owl the lives of her young, as story-tellers, among them La Fontaine, the seventeenth-century fabulist, have recounted: One day, as she left her nest in search of food, the owl asked the eagle, who was also hunting for food, to make sure that he did not eat her young. How was he to know which were hers, he asked. She replied that they were so beautiful, he could not mistake them. So, spotting some truly ugly, scrawny young birds, he ate them. When the owl returned, she found her nest empty. She complained bitterly to the eagle, who replied that she had only herself to blame for telling a lie; after all, had she not claimed that her young were beautiful?

Upon first seeing an owl, the shape of its head is its immediate distinguishing feature. How did the owl come to have such a strangely-shaped head?

An Eskimo legend tells how the Short-eared Owl was once a young girl who lived in a village beside a river. She was changed by magic into a bird with a long beak, and became so frightened that she flew up and

Snowy Owls by T.J. Greenwood.

away in a very erratic manner, and struck her face against the side of a house, flattening both her face and her beak.

From Burma there comes a different version of this story:

In the beginning of time, an assembly of birds was called to take decisions on some general principles. They invited a wise-looking owl to make a proclamation, whereupon he said: 'If there is to be light, may it be perpetual, or if there is to be darkness, may it last without end.' The birds were very angered at this proposition and they all jumped on the owl's head, flattening it, and the owl's head has been flattish ever since.

Anyone who has dissected an owl's head will be aware of the fact that there is an unusual bony structure surrounding the owl's eyeball. In a somewhat ghoulish claim, the Newuk Indians of California say this is made up of the fingernails of ghosts caught by the owl. The owl, it seems, has a predilection for human nails, for in northern China it was believed that the *hsiu-liu*, a small owl, used to enter houses at night and there gather human fingernails. By studying these carefully, the owl came to know the inhabitants of the house very well and would know which one to single out for its next fearsome visit.

In a Persian legend, however, the nails of a Zoroastrian which have had a spell cast over them are used as arrows by wizards and demons to attack and kill the owl. The only way the owl can save itself is to eat the nails.

The ghosts — or souls — of the dead in Russia in turn put to good use the owl's own powerful claws. These were carried around by hunters because it was believed that in the event of their death, their souls, in their wanderings, had to climb a steep mountain to reach heaven, and the owl's claws prevented them from sliding backwards.

Pen-and-ink drawing by David Pratt.

Two Little Owls by Winifred Austen.

Apart from the intense whiteness of the Snowy Owl, few owls have very striking plumage. Yet their rather drab colouring is an effective camouflage for the bird when it sits motionless during the day, blending so skilfully with its surroundings to become nearly invisible.

The Zuni Indians, however, have a fanciful explanation for the Burrowing Owl acquiring its speckled grey and white plumage. According to their folklore, the owls unintentionally spilled a white foam over themselves during one of their ceremonial dances whilst laughing helplessly at the antics and stupidity of a coyote that was trying to join in the dance.

Before the advent of photography, owls rarely posed long enough for artists to draw or paint them, and the majority of subjects for portraits were dead – and stuffed – or were drawn from memory. Several eighteenth-century English artist-naturalists mention finding their subjects in the collections of patrons and travellers.

Of the live birds painted, Eagle Owls were a popular subject for they seemed to tolerate captivity better than other species. However, George Edwards, a prolific eighteenth-century artist mentions a Great Horned Owl kept alive at the Mourning Bush Tavern by Aldersgate in London, and one of Eleazar Albin's models was a Little Owl which had been brought back to England by one 'Captain Boreman, it having lost its way at Sea, lighting on the Mast of the ship and was so tired that it suffered itself to be taken without any resistance, and was preserved and brought home by him, and given to me by his brother, Thomas Boreman, Bookseller on Ludgate Hill.' (*Natural History of Birds*, 1734).

It is likely that migrating owls swept ashore in gales were also a source of many of the stuffed specimens. Henry Seebohm, another British naturalist, this time of the nineteenth century, describes how a flock of Snowy Owls accompanied a ship halfway across the Atlantic, from the coast of Labrador to Ireland. On another occasion he himself stalked and shot down one such owl; the gale-lashed coastline of Sutherland was, it seems, a particularly good spot for such finds.

There is, even today, in London Zoo, a Snowy Owl which alighted upon a ship some years ago off the Azores, thousands of miles from its natural habitat. In recent years, owls have been tagged to check their migration patterns. A Burrowing Owl from Utah was later found in Baja, California, two Long-eared Owls from Saskatchewan and Michigan stopped over in southern Mexico, while one young Snowy

Owl from Cambridge Bay in Canada flew the amazing distance of three and a half thousand miles to Sakhalin in the Soviet Union.

Hunting & Hunted Owls

Many a naturalist has resorted to the chopping block to establish what the owl eats. Examination of the bird's stomach has provided varied and surprising results. John Gould, who studied the data amassed by Charles Darwin on *The Beagle* during his travels through the southern seas, reports that Mr Bynoe, the surgeon, killed an owl in the Clonos Archipelago, and upon opening up its stomach, he found it filled with the remains of large-sized crabs.

Eleazar Albin was also intrigued by the owl's eating habits, and on spotting an owl flying up and down at dusk, catching at the grass, he wrote: 'I desired my son, who was with me, to shoot him and when we dissected him I found in his stomach several of the white grass moths and other insects.' (*Natural History of Birds*, 1734).

John James Audubon, the nineteenth-century American artist and naturalist, did not resort to the scalpel, but merely observed a Snowy Owl 'lying flat and lengthwise with its head down near the water. One might have supposed the bird sound asleep. The instant the fish rose to the surface, the owl thrust out the claw that was next to the water, seized it, and drew it out like lightning.' (*Ornithological Biography*, 1831).

However, the majority of owls do feed at night on rodents, as Aristotle noted in his *History of Animals* (4th century BC): 'The owls ... procure their food by hunting in the night ... They do not do this all the night but in twilight and at early dawn. They hunt mice and lizards and beetles and other such small animals.'

Some owls obviously have a premonition of a good meal, as was reported in 1580: 'An army of mice so overran the marshes near Southminster that they ate up the grass to the very roots ... But at length a great number of strange painted owls came and devoured the mice.'

The massing of owls has been noted quite frequently. Thomas Bewick, the eighteenth-century English engraver, noticed for instance twenty-eight Short-eared Owls in a turnip field. This recalls another owl in a turnip field who had a narrow, and lucky escape:

'One day Caleb caught sight of an odd-looking brownish-grey object out in the middle of the turnip-field, and as he looked it rose up two or three feet into the air, then dropped back again, and this curious

Opposite. Late twelfth-century copy of the *Commentary on the Apocalypse* by the eighth-century Spanish monk, Beatus. Two owls find room in the Ark, and join a collection of real and fabulous creatures saved from the waters of the Flood by Noah.

Page 40. Barn Owl by J.M.W. Turner, from an album of bird watercolours which Turner painted for the children of his close friend and patron, Walter Fawkes of Farnley Hall, Yorkshire, 1810–15.

'Lugubrious birds of the night, singing their funereal hymns.' G. Casti, *Animali Parlanti*, 18th century.

Late nineteenth-century ceramic owl
from the west of England.

Drawn from Nature by A. Wilson.   Engraved by A. Lawson.

Opposite. Great Horned Owl and Barn Owl by Alexander Wilson, *American Ornithology*, 1812.

movement was repeated at intervals of two or three minutes until he went to see what the thing was. It turned out to be a long-eared owl, with its foot accidentally caught by a slack thread, which allowed the bird to rise a couple of feet into the air; but every such attempt to escape ended in its being pulled back to the ground again. It was excessively lean, so weightless in his hand, when he took it up after disengaging its foot, that he thought it must have been captive for the space of two or three days. The wonder was that it had kept alive during those long

Sketch of an owl by Carl Linnaeus, the Swedish naturalist. At the age of twenty-five, Linnaeus travelled to Lapland where he shot down this bird at night, without dismounting from his trotting horse. He later sketched it in his journal. Throughout his life many of his drawings retained this child-like quality.

Owl and Bees by Joseph Crawhall, a late nineteenth-century artist associated with the Glasgow School of Painters. Mary Auras, to whom the sketch is dedicated, was a German lady for whom Crawhall had a secret admiration. Alas, she married someone else!

'Among the Creek [Indians] . . . the junior priests . . . constantly wear a white mantle, and have a Great [Horned] Owl skin cased and stuffed very ingeniously, so well executed as almost to appear like the living bird, having large sparkling glass beads, or buttons, fixed in the head for eyes.' William Bartram, *Travels*, 1794.

midsummer days of intolerable heat out there in the middle of the burning field. Yet it was in very fine feather and beautiful to look at with its long, black ear-tufts and round, orange-yellow eyes, which would never lose their fiery lustre until glazed in death. Caleb's first thought on seeing it closely was that it would have been a prize to anyone who liked to have a handsome bird stuffed in a glass cage. Then raising it over his head he allowed it to fly, whereupon it flew off a distance of a dozen or fifteen yards, and pitched among the turnips after which it ran a little space and rose again with labour, but soon recovering strength it flew away over the field and finally disappeared in the deep shade of the copse beyond.'

(W.H. Hudson, *A Shepherd's Life*, 1910)

Stuffed Horned Owl.

Due to its partiality to rodents, and sometimes to the superstitions surrounding it, the owl has often been considered a welcome visitor to farms and gardens. Charles Waterton, the nineteenth-century English traveller and naturalist, who established the first bird sanctuary in

England at his home at Walton Hall in Yorkshire, decided while in Rome during the winter of 1840–1 to take a number of Little Owls home with him, saying they would be 'peculiarly useful to the British horticulturalist ... in his kitchen garden.' Those that survived the journey, however, had wider ambitions, for they all disappeared without trace into the wilds of Yorkshire.

The presence of owls in the fields was a boon for farmers, no doubt scaring away those notorious early harvesters – the rabbits. In the district of Léon in Britanny the farmers regarded the owl as auspicious and told that if you spotted one in a field on your way to harvest you were assured of a good crop.

Transylvanian farmers, on the other hand, took a dim view of the owl. Mindful, perhaps, of Count Dracula's many disguises, they scared the owls away, it was rumoured, by walking around their fields, naked.

The owl's ability to keep down the rodent population was appreciated in other parts of Europe, where farmers would build owl-holes into the eaves of their barns to encourage the birds to nest there. One tame pair of Barn Owls in Norfolk kept watch from the rafters during harvest and threshing time, swooping down when they spotted a mouse in a sheaf, and carrying it off in their claws. If farmers did not attract sufficient numbers of live owls they sometimes resorted to burying or hanging dead owls at the doors of their barns to deter mice and rats. The Rev. Gilbert White reported the strange occurrence of a pair of swallows building their nest on the wings and body of a dead owl.

Small rodents are usually thought of as the common prey of the owl, yet the bird will equally pursue creatures at least as large as itself, even at the risk of losing its own life. John Macoun, observing the Horned Owl in Canada noted:

'I think hares are its chief food during the winter. It also kills a good many skunks in summer. On one occasion my brothers found one that had seized a skunk which had bitten it so badly that it died from its wounds. It kills muskrats in the fall when they are building their houses ... and one night two winters ago, one came into the barnyard and killed two geese. The farmer caught it in a trap a few nights later.'
(John Macoun, *Catalogue of Canadian Birds*, 1909)

Ulisse Aldrovandi, *Ornithologiae*, 1599.

On the other hand, if food is more easily available, the owl will not scorn it. The Rev. F.O. Morris, a renowned nineteenth-century naturalist, remembered hearing of one owl which would enter a cottage the minute the family sat down to a meal and would place itself on the back of a chair or on the table and share in the meal.

It might appear, to the casual owl-watcher, that the country clergy of eighteenth- and nineteenth-century England spent their entire working life observing the bird life of their parishes. Certainly what spare time they did have was filled with letter-writing and diary-keeping. Having observed for some time the feeding and nesting habits of a pair of White Owls which were breeding under the eaves of his church, the Rev. Gilbert White wrote in a letter dated July 8, 1773:

'About an hour before sunset ... they sally forth in quest of prey ... I have minuted these birds with my watch for an hour together, and have found that they return to their nest, the one or the other of them about once in five minutes ... As they take their prey with their claws, so they

Salt-glazed stoneware vase manufactured by the Martin Brothers, 1876.

carry it in their claws to their nest; but, as the feet are necessary in the ascent under the tiles, they constantly perch first on the roof of the chancel, and shift the mouse from their claws to their bill, that their feet may be at liberty to take hold of the plate on the wall as they are rising under the eaves.'

(Rev. Gilbert White, *The Natural History of Selbourne*, 1789)

In a subsequent letter he noted that '... the young of the Barn owl will eat indiscriminately all that is brought: snails, rats, kittens, puppies, magpies, and any kind of carrion or offal.'

The owl's varied hunting habits happily provided the flamboyant Huey Long who was Governor of Louisiana in the 1930s, with a metaphor describing the tactics of his two political opponents – Herbert Hoover (the hoot owl) and Theodore Roosevelt (the scrootch owl) [sic]:

'A hoot owl bangs into the roost and knocks the hen clean off, and catches her while she's falling. But a scrootch owl slips into the roost and scrootches up to a hen and talks softly to her. And the hen just falls in love with him, and the first thing you know, there ain't no hen.'

The fearless night-hunter has difficulties, however, when it emerges by day, having to contend with attacks by other birds. Henry Seebohm was told of a Little Owl in the Netherlands which had been released after capture, but '... she had scarcely got more than forty yards from us when she was pursued by a mob of starlings, swallows and other birds, from whom she soon took refuge in a chestnut tree, to the evident annoyance of a chaffinch, who immediately began to "spink, spink" in a most excited way.' (Quoted in Rev. F.O. Morris, *History of British Birds*, 1851).

Pliny noticed this mobbing of the owl by smaller birds, but had great faith in the owl's ability to defend itself:

'The owlet shows considerable shrewdness in its engagement with other birds; for when surrounded by too great a number, it throws itself on its back, and so, resisting with its feet and rolling up puts its body into a mass, defends itself with the beak and talons; until the hawk, attracted by a certain natural affinity, comes to its assistance and takes its share in the combat.'

(Pliny, *Natural History*, 1st century AD)

Allegorical stories based on the enmity between the smaller birds and the owl are worldwide and found in works as varied as Aesop's fables,

Woodcut of Barn Owl by Harold
Cook.

Opposite. Medieval bench-end at
Rimpton, Somerset.

Opposite. Fourteenth-century
misericord in Gloucester Cathedral.

the fables of La Fontaine, and in the Indian *Panchatantra*. In the Middle Ages, the mobbing of the owl was used as a symbol of the Jews being persecuted by Christians. A twelfth-century bestiary notes:

'... the owl Noctua is so called because it flies at night. It cannot see by day because its sight is weakened by the splendour of the rising sun. Owls ... represent the Jews, who refuse redemption.'

The natural mobbing – or 'astonishing', as Aristotle put it – of the owl by smaller birds was put to good use by hunters and fowlers:

'... during the day other birds fly round the owl, which is called astonishing it, and as they fly around, pluck off its feathers. For this reason fowlers use it in hunting for all kinds of birds.'
(Aristotle, *History of Animals*, 4th century BC)

Opposite. Chained Eagle Owl.

Using the owl as a bait has been a widespread practice for centuries and there are many medieval illuminated manuscripts and wood carvings that show the owl being hunted – often being shot at by an archer or a peasant – or being attacked by smaller birds as it sits tied to a pole, a helpless decoy. One famous owner of owls was the Emperor Frederick II Hohenstaufen of Sicily, an avid sportsman and hunter, whose treatise *On the Art of Hunting with Birds* displayed his detailed knowledge – and love – of birds. He always took falcons with him on his travels, but when he arrived in Ravenna in northern Italy in November 1231 his exotic menagerie also included 'Bearded owls'.

Owls were clearly still widely used as bait in the nineteenth century, as Charles de Kay relates after a visit to Rome:

'I came upon a seller of owls, poor fellows, fastened securely to the top of the pole by one foot. Every now and then one would flutter helplessly, hanging by the leg. In such guise they are in demand as lures for small birds, which hate them so bitterly that they are readily inveigled into traps or into limed twigs.'
(Charles de Kay, *Bird Gods of Ancient Europe*, 1898)

And in a book published at the beginning of this century in Spain by the Duke of Medinaceli the use of live or stuffed Eagle Owls as bait was still being advocated. This makes the tale of Aesop's prophetic owl all the more poignant:

'The owl in her wisdom once counselled the birds, long ago, when the first oaks sprouted in the forest, to pull them up out of the ground: "you see this tiny tree? If you take my advice, destroy it now while it is small; for when it grows big, mistletoe will appear on it, and from it birdlime will be prepared in order to ensnare you." Again when the first seed of flax appeared, she said: "go and eat that seed, for it is the seed of the flax from which men will one day make nets in which you will be caught." Lastly, when she saw the first archer, she warned the birds that he was their worst enemy who would make darts, armed with their own feathers, which would fly faster than the birds themselves, and which would kill them. But the birds took no notice of what the owl said: in fact, they thought she was mad and laughed at her. But when they discovered that all her words turned out to be true, they changed their

minds and wondered at her knowledge, and considered her the wisest of birds. And whenever she appears, the birds now wait on her in the hope of hearing something that may be for their own good. But she no longer gives them advice, but in solitude laments their past follies.'

The downfall of both owls and small birds at the hand of man – the one to be used as a bait for the other – was used by Leonardo da Vinci in his *Notebooks* as a cautionary tale on the identity of one's true enemies:

'The thrushes were overjoyed on seeing a man catch the owl and take away her freedom by binding her feet with strong bonds. But then by means of bird lime the owl was the cause of the thrushes losing not only their liberty but even their lives. This is said of those states which rejoice at seeing their rulers lose their liberty, whereafter they lose hope and remain bound in the powers of their enemy, losing their liberty and often their lives.'

Japanese watercolour.

The owl is by no means a timid bird and owls cornered in the wild have often displayed startling ferocity and cunning. One particular female Eagle Owl, in her fury, inspired a lyricism rarely found in a naturalist's description:

'The female is a third larger than the male, and far surpasses him in every manly quality. She takes the lead throughout; she is everywhere and everything; he nowhere and nothing. Her talons have a terrible grip and strength. When she is angered . . . she lowers her head almost to the ground, moves it slowly from side to side in a long sweep, snaps loudly with her bill, quivers from head to foot with half-suppressed rage, and raises her wings in a vast circle above her body, each particular feather standing on end, erect and distinct, her eyes flashing fiercely the while, and turning from a yellow to a fiery red.'
(R.B. Smith, *Bird Life and Bird Lore*, 1905)

Similarly, the Canadian naturalist, John Macoun, recounted how Snowy Owls, perched on ice floes, would try to keep out of range of the gun fire and, when wounded, so terrified the dogs, who could not then get close enough to catch the owls. An example of the bird's cunning was described by Alexander Wilson, the nineteenth-century American naturalist. The bird, an Eagle Owl with a broken wing, had

52

been nursed for some days by a farmer, and then it disappeared. After this, almost daily, a chicken would disappear from the roost until only a few were left:

'... The fox, mink and weasel were alternately the reputed authors of this mischief, until one morning, the old lady herself, rising before the day to bake, in passing towards the oven, surprised her late prisoner the Owl regaling himself on the body of a newly killed hen! The thief instantly made for a hole under the house, from whence the enraged matron dislodged him with a brush handle, and without mercy despatched him ...'

(Alexander Wilson, *American Ornithology*, 1824)

The ferocity and cunning of the owl is matched only by its concern for its young: if the owl caught happens to be a young bird, the parents frequently mourn it, and try to retrieve it. Failing that, they at least feed it, as one observer recalled:

'... on the summit eagle owls had built their nest. One day in July, a young bird barely fledged was caught by servants and shut up in a large hen coop. On the following morning, a young partridge was found lying dead near the door of the coop; and night after night, for fourteen days, the same mark of attention was repeated. The gentleman and his servant watched for several nights in order that they might observe through the

Owl mobbed by birds, from *Birds and Beasts* by Francis Barlow, 1775.

53

window when and how this supply was brought; but in vain, though there could be no doubt that the parents of the bird were the caterers.'
(W. Macgilivray, *History of British Birds*, 1840)

Another naturalist made a similar observation:

'... a servant [at Walton Hall] robbed the [owl's] nest and placed the young ones in a willow cage not far from the hollow tree. The parent birds brought food for their captive offspring, but not being able to get it through the bars of the cage, they left it on the ground outside. It consisted of mice, rats, small birds and fish.'
(Charles Waterton, *Essays on Natural History*, 1838)

The truth of the matter, the truth of the matter –
As one who supplies us with hats is a Hatter,
As one who is known for his growls is a Growler –
My Grandpa traps owls, yes, my grandpa's an Owler.
'Owls are such sages,' he says, 'I surmise
Listening to owls could make the world wise.'
Nightlong his house is shaken with hoots,
And he wakes to owls in his socks and his boots.
Owls, owls, nothing but owls,
The most fantastical of fowls:
White owls from the Arctic, black owls from the Tropic.
Some are far-sighted, others myopic.
There are owls on his picture frames, owls on his chairs,
Owls in dozens ranked on his stairs.
Eyes, eyes, rows of their eyes.
Some are big as collie dogs, some are thumbsize.
(Ted Hughes, *My Grandpa*, 1961)

Superstitions surrounding the owl include some on the hunting and trapping of owls. Sadly for the owls, Grandpa in Ted Hughes' poem did not live in Illinois, for there people believed that if an owl were harmed or killed, revenge would be taken on the sportsman's family – one of them would be badly injured or killed.
In parts of England and Germany, killing an owl was also considered to be unlucky, although in the fens of East Anglia or in the bogs of

Noctua by J.G. Keulemans in H.E. Dresser, *History of the Birds of Europe*, 1871–81.

54

Nineteenth-century carving in lime wood.

Ireland, owls were beaten to death if spotted and caught just the same, and the youths of Bury St Edmunds in Suffolk traditionally set out on Christmas Day in the hope of potting an owl, although the predictability of the hunt should have forewarned the owls to keep out of sight on that day. In the west of England, on February 14, St Valentine's Day, owls and sparrows formed a vital part of the procession that wound its way from village to village — though whether to be offered as love potions, or for some other reason altogether is not known.

The reasons for the hunting and persecution of owls are often sound, if questionable. Perhaps the owl's 'scarcity value' increased interest in having one, stuffed, sitting on a bookshelf as a conversation piece, and certainly if your next meal was intended to consist of a small bird, the owl served its purpose, rather like a rabbit trap. Equally likely, however, is that the owl itself was intended for the pot, in one form or another. Aristotle mentions that several species of owl 'are eatable and highly esteemed' and we know that owl was eaten in ancient Babylon. Indeed, recent archaeological finds in China, both written evidence on bamboo slips and painted scenes on murals, have shed light on eating habits during the Han period. It seems that baked owl was a delicacy served at Han feasts and was much enjoyed by the wealthy urban dwellers. A Ming dynasty source also mentions owls as a delicacy, and in present-day China, owls can be purchased at food markets, along with monkeys, scorpions and cockroaches.

Pair of Chinese earthenware bottles with detachable heads, found among tomb furnishings, Han dynasty, 202 BC–220 AD.

The French eighteenth-century naturalist, Georges Louis Leclerc, Comte de Buffon, may also have been a gourmet, for he tells us that 'white owls are not bad to eat at about three weeks, for they are fat and well fed', and the Creoles of Louisiana, perhaps inheriting dishes from French *cuisine*, used to eat Barred Owl – but since no recipes have been handed down we can only surmise whether the bird was roasted or put in a stew. We do know that in parts of Yorkshire it was made into a soup, said to cure whooping cough; but it was hunger pure and simple that drove Thomas Nuttall, the American naturalist and one-time Harvard teacher, to eat an owl while on one of his last expeditions in the mountains of north-west America. He was obviously ready to agree with the old New England saying 'I'm hungry enough to eat a boiled owl!'

Not everyone finds eating owl agreeable, however, although perhaps it was the way in which it was prepared that resulted in the bad stomach pains suffered by people in Morocco who, thereafter, said that the very smell of owl brought on a recurrence of these pains. In Picardy, in northern France, a more sinister ill-effect – deranging of the mind – was believed to be caused by eating owl's eggs. According to the Judeo-Christian tradition the owl's meat-eating habits made it unclean, as the Old Testament states: '... And these are they which ye shall have in abomination among the fowls; they shall not be eaten ... the white owl ... and the horned owl.' (Leviticus). It has been claimed, nonetheless, that 'unclean' animals and birds in Jewish orthodox thought were in fact sacred, and were linked with deities in ancient religions and rituals.

Opposite. Tawny Owl by Robert Gillmor.

56

Owls – or their eggs – not served up at the family meal were likely to end up in the medicine cupboard instead and there are many examples of the folk cures they were used for. The Greek, Philostratus, mentions that an owl egg, if made into a soup as the moon was waning, was a cure for the falling sickness; if given to children, it ensured them life-long temperance and sobriety (the owl, being associated with Athene, was considered wise and temperate).

Other variations on curing drunkenness have also been recorded. John Swan in his *Speculum Mundi*, published in 1635, suggested that 'the egges of an owl broken and put into the cup of a drunkard, or one disirous to follow drinking, will so work on him that he will suddenly lothe his good liquor and be displeased with drinking.' The instructions in the Gironde in France were even more precise: an omelette had to be made of five, nine or thirteen owls' eggs; only then would it cure a man

Above. Eighteenth-century silver toothpick-holder.

Late nineteenth-century silver-mounted pepperettes in their original box. Silver 'table-toys' were particularly popular in the latter half of the nineteenth century in England and their range was endless.

Opposite. The Owl and the Pussycat by Fred Aris.

Pussy said to the Owl, 'You elegant fowl,
How charmingly sweet you sing!'

(From *The Owl and the Pussycat*, Edward Lear)

Stained glass panel, *The Nativity* by John Piper, 1982. This work was inspired by paintings in typical late medieval style on a partition at Shulbrede Priory in West Sussex.

Opposite. Juvenile Little Owl by Benjamin Perkins, painted for the birth of a friend's son, George Burton.

A wise bird by all men I'm reckoned
For I can tell all things to happen:
Of hunger and of war I know
And who long life will live to show;
I know if woman loves her man
And when misfortune comes to damn;
I know whose life will be forfeit
And who a wretched death will meet;
In battle, when the sides do clash
I know which army makes a dash;
In spring I know which herbs and trees
Will sprout and blossom to give ease;
I can foretell which homes will crumble
And whether men will strive or tumble;
I know when ships in oceans founder
And when foul weather tears land
    assunder;
Of many things I know much more,
For I have much of learned lore.
(From *The Owl and the Nightingale*,
attributed to Nicholas de Guildford,
late 12th century).

Benjamin Perkins 1989.

BUBO MAXIMUS, *Sibb*

J Wolf and H.C.Richter del. et lith.

Walter Imp.

les actus pectoris bene agentes repre
fluatem dampnant. infeliz q bubo di
t ea que pdirm' opatur.
ra
gu
li
a
uo
r
u
li
eils importunu quod ut philosophoz
tate.ut hereticoz uibofitate gloriam sig

Above. Detail from a
mid-thirteenth-century English
bestiary.

of drunkenness. The advanced stages of drinking, and gout, could also
be cured — with salted owl, though this delicacy no doubt induced
further thirst, Amusingly, there is a Polish tale with a rather fine twist
that tells of an owl who became so drunk at a wedding, and behaved so
badly, that he was ostracised by all the other birds — and this is another
reason why the owl is now persecuted by them.

Fashion-conscious members of the family, at the first sign of grey
hairs, could also use an owl's egg to darken the offending strands —
presumably by applying the sticky mess to their head; and dandruff
could also be cured, according to the Shoshone Indians: all you had to
do was to put your head inside the burrow of a Ground Owl and shake
your head!

Owl feathers were also of use to men: the people of Sieradz in Poland
believed that, burnt over charcoal, they were good for rheumatism

Opposite. Eagle Owl by Josef Wolf
from *Birds of Great Britain* by John
Gould, 1862–73.

Chinese wine vessel and cover, cast on
either side with a large owl, Shang
dynasty, 1600–1027 BC.

(though baked owl served the same purpose), and the Pima Indians claimed that waving them over people who were wasting away, or suffering from fits and trances, was an effective cure.

Folk remedies such as these survive and reappear throughout the world and at different times. How we all happen to hold similar beliefs about parts of the owl's anatomy is partially a mystery, although in some cases the transfer of such beliefs is easy to trace: for instance, many of those held in medieval Europe originated in Greece and Rome, and those held in North America would have travelled to that continent with, say, the slaves of Africa, and, later, with European immigrants.

For the ever-superstitious Romans, Pliny compiled the following list of potential owl cures, carefully prefacing his remarks with 'Let the following stand as a remarkable proof of the frivolous nature of the magic art.' They include:

Owl tapestry by C.F.A. Voysey, an English textile designer of the turn of the century and a prominent member of the Arts and Crafts Movement.

The remedy for ear-ache: . . . by injecting into the ear an owlet's brain or liver, mixed with oil, or by applying the mixture to the partoid gland.

Remedy for affection of the sinews: . . . ashes of the head of a horned owl, taken in honied wine with a lily root.

Methods for arresting haemorrage: . . . the bird known as the screech owl is boiled in oil, ewe milk butter and honey being added to the preparation when properly dissolved.

(Pliny, *Natural History*, 1st century AD)

In view of the owl's many attractions for mankind – as bait, or food, or folk remedy – it is hardly surprising that the owl retreated to deserted places and hid in ruins and spots made inaccessible by brambles and nettles:

> Before the tombs the thorns grew rank and foul,
> No man may pass unless he hews a road.
> And on a plum tree growing near, the owl
> Has chosen her abode.
>
> (from the *Shih Ching*, compiled by Confucius)

The desert also made a good hiding place, according to Pliny, for it was 'horribly hard of access'. Hollow trees, uninhabited by other birds, were also favoured, but ruins of houses and palaces, long abandoned by man and beast, were probably the best of all. And rather than being apologetic about the state of his dwelling, one owl proudly claimed he was:

'. . . of a very ancient and extensive family, though rather fallen into decay, [who] possess ruinous castles and palaces in all parts of Spain. There is scarcely a tower of the mountains, or a fortress of the plain, or an old citadel of a city, but has some brother, or uncles or cousins quartered in it . . .'

(Washington Irving, *Tales of the Alhambra*, 1832)

And then, of course, there was the church tower, particularly coveted by the White Owl. No one would surely dare to disturb an owl in such a holy place – which is why, according to a Flemish legend, the priest offered the tower to the owls, in exchange for their services in getting rid of rats and mice. However, the White Owl's nightly forays, and its hisses and snorts amongst the tangle of tombs, convinced the villagers of one English parish that their graveyard was full of spectres and goblins. Even educated people could feel uneasy: Carl Linnaeus, the eighteenth-century Swedish naturalist, described in the journal he kept while travelling through southern Sweden, that the owls at night '... shrieked like ghosts.'

Churches and temples are both sanctuaries, and, according to a Japanese legend, the forests near Buddhist temples have been a haven for owls ever since Fukuro, the owl, was attacked by the eagle and all the other birds, when they found out about his love for Uso-dori, the bullfinch. Fukuro was so distressed at the death of his beloved during the attack that he donned monastic robes and has roamed the country as an itinerant monk ever since.

There is another very good reason for the owl choosing distant and lonesome places to live, for the owl has a reputation for kidnapping and even killing children. Spine-chilling stories were told to naughty children by the Wishram Indians of Washington about the old she-owl who snatched children away, and many other Indian peoples would warn children that if they did not behave they would be taken away by the owl – much the same as European children are frightened with the witch. One such Apache story had a happy ending: one of their legendary monsters was the Big Owl who carried off children, but in a series of encounters he was outwitted by man and finally destroyed.

Possibly the most colourful kidnapping story comes from the Shoshone Indians: four young children were being pursued by the evil owl, but a buffalo calf saw what was happening and protected the children. As the owl approached the calf, behind which the children were cowering, the calf put its head down and tossed the owl straight up into the sky, so far that he landed on the moon – where you can still see him sitting ... And in another imaginative turn of mind, the Laksamshu Indians of British Columbia, who have an owl as their creator, explained that the pitted lands in which they lived were formed when the owl was trying to dig holes to hide a small boy whom it had kidnapped.

There have also been a few stories of man-eating owls – their diet primarily made up of young children. In parts of China and Malaya it was believed that owls were particularly partial to the blood of newly-born infants, and there are several North American Indian tales of children being taken away and eaten. In Fez, in Morocco, small children were not allowed to play outside after dusk in case an owl flew over them and made them seriously ill.

Some years ago, a 'Wanted alive' poster was used in England by the Royal Society for the Protection of Birds. It was not in connection with the owl's kidnapping activities, however. On the contrary, it was an attempt to make the public more aware of the owl's own plight and its

Japanese wood *netsuke* (toggle), signed
Tomokazu, 19th century.

WANTED — ALIVE!

THE BARN - OWL

Last heard of in nearly every country parish. Occupation, rodent destroyer. Reward
for sparing its life—more food for humans! Protected by law! Know your friends,
preserve the countryside and its birds, and support the ROYAL SOCIETY FOR THE

PROTECTION OF BIRDS

82 VICTORIA STREET, LONDON, S.W.1

Japanese *inro* (small box). It was hung
over the *obi* – the wide sash worn with
the kimono. The *inro* was used as a
'pocket'. Attached by a cord to it and
acting as a counterweight, was a
netsuke (see above).

dwindling population. There was particular concern over the rapidly
diminishing numbers of Barn Owls. The campaign proved to be most
effective, and a number of police stations around the country were soon
being presented with live Barn Owls.

Another 'Wanted' advertisement, but this time completely baffling,
appeared in the English press in 1905:

Wanted at once by a London firm: 1,000 owls.

No box number, no name, and no reason given.

Early fourteenth-century manuscript. The detail shows an ape gazing at an owl's urine specimen bottle – a widely used method of diagnosing an illness.

WITCHES & WIZARDS

Prehistoric cave painting at Trois Frères, France.

Kill the owl-sorcerer, the owlet-sorcerer, the dog-sorcerer,
the cuckoo-sorcerer, the eagle-sorcerer, the vulture-sorcerer.
Indra, crush the demon to powder as if with a mill stone.

(from the *Rig Veda*)

The owl has had a long and varied association with witches and magic: 'All birds hate owls. People hate owls, too. Owls are connected with witches' – so runs an old Zuni Indian saying. Many of these beliefs must stem from the owl's night-time appearances – and sudden disappearances – in the gloom. But there is also something rather uncannily human about the face of the Barn Owl, for instance – a resemblance that is somewhat disturbing: could 'human' witches and owls be inter-

Contemporary American metal sculpture.

Blue-eyed, strange-voiced, sharp-beaked,
   ill-omened fowl,
What art thou?
What I ought to be – an owl.
(James Montgomery, *Birds*, 19th century)

Opposite. L'Hibou by Bernard Buffet, 1958.

changeable? Traditionally, owls sometimes provided the witch with a means of transport when a broom was not available, but, in some cases, the witch developed wings and flew away herself.

70

Page 72. Mid-nineteenth-century Japanese watercolour from *Studies of Flowers, Birds etc.*

A chilling tale of the owl was recorded in Peking in 1755. It was noticed that a large number of young children died of convulsions and the story goes that, during their attacks:

'... a bird like an owl was seen to hover round the lamps in the sick room. At the death of the child, the bird vanished. An archer, determined to get to the bottom of the mystery, went to the room of a sick child and when the bird appeared, he shot it. Crying out with pain, the bird disappeared out of the window. It was traced by its blood to a little room near the kitchen of a military officer called Li. There lay an old woman with green eyes, wounded in the loins by an arrow. She was of the country of Niao Tzu, a non-Chinese mountain people of the south, and had been captured by Li in one of his campaigns in Yun-Nan. She had long been suspected of witchcraft, and confessed she could turn herself into a bird of prey. In that form she sallied forth about midnight to feed upon the brains of infants. She had thus caused the death of more than a hundred. She was burnt alive, and the epidemic of convulsions ceased.'

(G. Willoughby-Meade, *Chinese Ghouls and Goblins*, 1928)

A version of this story was already circulating in ancient Rome, as Apuleius recounts in *The Golden Ass*. However, such transformations were no easy undertaking:

'One day, Fotsis came running to me in great feare, and said that her mistress, to worke her sorceries on such as she loved, intended the night following to transform herself into a bird and to fly whither she pleased. Wherefore she willed me privily to prepare myself to see the same. And when midnight came she led me softly into a high chamber and bid me look through the chink in the doore: where first I saw how she put off all her garments and took out of a certain coffer sundry kindes of Boxes, of which she opened one, and tempered the ointment therein with her fingers, and then rubbed her body therewith from the sole of her foot to the crowne of the head, and when she had spoken privily with herself, having the candle in her hand, she shaked the parts of her body and became like an owle. Then she screeched like a Bird of that kind, and willing to prove her force, moved herself from the ground little by little, till at last she flew quite away.'

Page 73. Contemporary French cast iron sculpture.

Opposite. Tawny Owl by Moonlight, Graham Rust, 1984.

John Swan was telling his readers in 1635 that 'some, in old times, fabled such strange things of this bird, namely that it sucked out the blood of infants lying in their cradles, or changed their favours; whereupon some have used the same word for a witch, a fairee or hag.'

(*Speculum Mundi*). Some twenty years earlier, in the county of Leicestershire, the following testimony was given at the trial of three women suspected of witchcraft:

'She [Joan Willimott] and Joan and Margaret Flower had met in Blackburn Hill, the week before Joan's apprehension; and she had seen in Joan's house two spirits, the one like a rat, the other like an owl, and one of them had sucked her under her left ear.'

(Flower Trial, 1618–19)

That the owl was the witch's accomplice, closely associated with her fearful activities, was a commonly held belief in many parts of the world. In New Mexico, the hoot of an owl gave warning that the witches were approaching, and it was believed that there was a school of witches where every new apprentice, when first entering their cave, was taught – among other things – to transform herself into an owl. In Madagascar, the owl was said to join the witches as they danced on the graves of the dead. In Europe, the brothers Grimm fantasised in a fairy tale (presumably for children) about an owl which flew into a thicket and emerged as 'a crooked old woman, yellow and spindly, with round red eyes and a nose which reached to her chin.' If an owl was caught in West Africa, where it was also believed to be a witch's messenger, it had its claws broken and was otherwise maltreated in the belief that its 'human' counterpart was suffering the same pain.

THE THREE WITCHES OF BELVOIR.

The three witches of Belvoir, Leicestershire.

Skating Owls by Abraham Bloemaert, a Dutch early seventeenth-century painter and engraver. A sixteenth-century Dutch proverb stated that 'the world goes on skates,' meaning that the world slides and skids helplessly towards evil and wickedness. These two gruesome and self-assured skaters may have been leading the way.

To accomplish much of their mischief, witches often resorted to concocting magic potions, and owls were considered a vital ingredient. A voodoo brew from New Orleans sounds distinctly ghoulish and noxious:

'Take a dried one-eyed toad, a dried lizard, the little finger of a person who committed suicide, the wings of a bat, the eyes of a cat, the liver of an owl, and reduce all to powder. Then cut into fine pieces the lock of hair from a dead child, and mix with the powder. Make a bag from a piece of sheet used as a shroud, put the mixture in it, and lay it on the pillow of the intended victim ... he will pine away and die.'

Canidia, the witch of the Roman poet Horace, ordered 'the eggs and plumes of the night screech owl, smeared with the toad's loathsome and malignant venom' to be thrown into a cauldron for her unfortunate victim. But Macbeth's three witches' potion is probably the best known of all:

Fillet of a fenny snake,
In the cauldron boil and bake;
Eye of newt, and toe of frog,
Wool of bat, and tongue of dog,
Adder's fork, and blind worm's sting,
Lizard's leg, and howlet's wing,
For a charm of powerful trouble,
Like a hell-broth boil and bubble.
(William Shakespeare, *Macbeth*)

Another Macbeth owl, undeterred by all the murder and mayhem around him, had the dubious distinction of being played by a cat, one of mehitabel's *beaux* – as recounted by archy, the cockroach who lived in the New York offices of the *Evening Sun*:

Olaus Magnus, *Historia de Gentibus Septentrionalibus*, 1555.

78

once i played the owl
in modejska s production
of macbeth
i sat above the castle gate
in the murder scene
and made my yellow
eyes shine through the dusk
like an owl s eyes
modejska was a real
trouper she knew how to pick
her support i would like
to see any of these modern
theatre cats play the owl s eyes
in modejska s lady macbeth
but they haven t got it nowadays
they haven t got it
here

(Don Marquis, *archy and mehitabel*,
1931)

Detail from a seventeenth-century
Bavarian manuscript.

Unlike witches, the medicine men of the North American Indians were a
highly respected group of men. They dispensed wisdom as well as
health-giving potions, they officiated at ceremonies and sacrifices, and
in many of these activities were accompanied by an owl in one form or
another. They carried stuffed owls, wore owl feathers, or sent prayers to
the owl, asking it for help in their enterprises – usually in a battle against

Shaman's (medicine man) charm, British Columbia, Queen Charlotte's Islands, early 19th century. Shamans performed curing rituals, using these charms which were often in the shape of birds or animals from which they derived their curing powers.

a neighbouring tribe.

The Kiowa Indians even believed that, after his death, a medicine man became an owl. Reporting to the American Bureau of Ethnology in 1917, J. Mooney explained:

'...a [Kiowa] medicine man derived his power from the body of an owl, wrapped in red cloth and decorated with various trinkets. This was kept constantly suspended from a tall pole set up in front of his tipi, and whenever at night the warning cry sounded from the thicket, he was accustomed to leave his place at the fire and go out, returning in a short while with a new revelation.'

In Europe, the wizard – a wise old man with magical powers – was probably the nearest counterpart to the medicine man. One magician in particular – Merlyn, the companion and advisor to the legendary King Arthur (Wart) when he was young – was always accompanied by the owl Archimedes, who perched on his shoulder, or kept otherwise at close range. Wart first met Archimedes when he went with Merlyn to his cavernous, cobwebby room:

'Merlyn took off his pointed hat when he came into this chamber, because it was too high for the roof, and immediately there was a scamper in one of the dark corners and a flap of soft wings, and a tawny owl sitting on the black skull-cap which protected the top of his head.
"Oh, what a lovely owl!" cried the Wart.
But when he went up to it and held out his hand, the owl grew half as tall again, stood up as stiff as a poker, closed its eyes so that there was only the smallest slit to peep through – as you are in the habit of doing when told to shut your eyes at hide-and-seek – and said in a doubtful voice: "There is no owl."
Then it shut its eyes entirely and looked the other way.
"It is only a boy," said Merlyn.
"There is no boy," said the owl hopefully, without turning round.
The Wart was so startled by finding that the owl could talk that he forgot his manners and came closer still. At this the bird became so nervous that it made a mess on Merlyn's head – the whole room was quite white with droppings – and flew off to perch on the farthest tip of the corkindrill's tail, out of reach.
"We see so little company," explained the magician, wiping his head with half a worn-out pair of pyjamas which he kept for that purpose, "that Archimedes is a little shy of strangers. Come, Archimedes, I want you to meet a friend of mine called Wart."'
(T.H. White, *The Once and Future King*, 1962)

HEARING, SEEING AN OWL

The first indication we usually have of an owl's presence is its cavernous hoot – unless it is the White Owl, which, according to R.B. Smith, '... screeches, snaps, snorts and hisses ...' but 'never hoots.' (*Bird Life and Bird Lore*, 1905)

In some parts of the world it is considered important to count the

Etching of Short-eared Owl by William Geldart.

Opposite. Winter Sunset with Barn Owl, painting by Raymond Booth, 1980.

Seventeenth-century Indian Mogul painting by Manohar – a painter at the court of Emperor Jahangir.

Page 84. Female Snowy Owl by Barry Driscoll.

Page 85. A rare large (14·5 cm) Ural Owl by Carl Fabergé, of black-speckled grey granite with diamond eyes, a gold beak and gold claws.

Opposite. Contemporary American batik picture.

number of hoots – or screeches. In southern India it was believed that:

'. . . one owl screech foretells death; two screeches, success in an under-taking; three, the arrival – by marriage – of a girl in the family; four, a disturbance; five, that the hearer will travel; six foretell the arrival of guests; seven, mental distress; eight, sudden death; and nine signify favourable results.'

However, you could never be sure, for in Adams Country in Illinois, one owl 'holler' meant that one person was about to rob you, and two 'hollers' meant that you would be robbed by two people. The Asinai Indians of Texas, on the other hand, had no need to count, for to them the owl was such a friend that whenever they heard it they would simply shout for joy. For the Black women of Louisiana an owl hoot did not mean joy, but simply that a visitor was arriving and they had to prepare more food.

The owl hoot has a strange, sad quality about it. Pliny called it 'a certain groan of doleful moaning', and it inspired R.C. Trevelyan to write some very moving lines:

From time to time an owl hoots in the distance.
He hoots not for me, I know;
Yet he seems to be uttering some deep meaning, some passionate
   wisdom.
Was it by such-like solemn shuddering cries
That our own remote forefathers before the birth of language
Communed with one another speechlessly,
Uttering their solitary moods of grief and joy and exultation?'
     (R.C. Trevelyan, *An Owl at Night*, early 20th
     century)

But, as we know, not all owls hoot, and John James Audubon was intrigued by the Saw-whet Owl, whose notes:

'. . . bear a great resemblance to the noise produced by filing the teeth of a large saw. On one particular occasion, while walking near my sawmill in Pennsylvania, to see that all was right there, I was much astonished to hear these sounds issuing from the interior of the grist-mill. The door having been locked, I had to go to my miller's house close by, to inquire if anyone was at work in it. He, however, informed me that the sounds I had heard were merely the note of what he called the Screech owl, whose nest was close by, in a hollow tree, deserted by the wood ducks . . .'

     (John James Audubon, *Ornithological Biography*,
     1831)

How, then, do owls come to have such a strange voice? The Algonquin Indians believed that it was the cry of the lovelorn owl for his lost, young and beautiful fish-hawk wife. But according to an old Louisiana tale, the cuckoo, that notorious trickster, was the cause: when Mr Owl was young, he could sing to beat all the other birds in the woods, and he even taught singing. He and Miss Owl lived in a respectable nest-house. One night, Miss Owl went out and told Mr Owl to stay home and mind the nest and the little ones. But as soon as she had gone, he took out his fiddle, and went out too. No sooner had he left than Miss Cuckoo, seeing a high-quality empty nest-house, laid an egg there. When Miss Owl returned home she wanted to know where this new egg had come

Eagle Owl by Edward Lear from *Birds of Europe* by John Gould, 1832–7. Lear, a very young man at the time, was engaged in painting the animals at the private zoo at Knowsley Hall in Lancashire, the home of the Earl of Derby. It was there that Lear embarked on his other, more famous career, as a writer of nonsense verses and limericks.

from, but Mr Owl had no idea, so Miss Owl threw him out, and he went in search of the bird who had laid the egg and brought about his misfortune. He wandered the world, sadly asking everywhere he went 'who, who', for so long that he forgot how to sing, and now all he can say is 'who, who'.

Whatever the origin of the owl's cry, it has frightened, perturbed and fascinated all who have heard it over the centuries. Travelling through the remote American countryside at the beginning of the last century, Alexander Wilson became used to the cries of the owl, but still experienced some disquiet:

'Along the mountainous shores of Ohio, and amidst the deep forests of Indiana, alone and reposing in the woods, this ghostly watchman has frequently warned me of the approach of morning and amazed me with his singular exclamations, sometimes sweeping down and around my

Ulisse Aldrovandi, *Ornithologiae*, 1599.

90

fire, uttering a loud and sudden Waugh O! Waugh O! sufficient to have alarmed a whole garrison. He has other nocturnal solos, no less melodious, one of which very strangely resembles the half-suppressed scream of a person being suffocated, or throttled, and cannot fail of being exceedingly entertaining to a lonely, benighted traveller in the midst of an Indian wilderness ...'

(Alexander Wilson, *American Ornithology*, 1804–14)

There have been many superstitious interpretations of the owl's hoot in various parts of the world. The Takelma Indians took the owl hoot as a sign of approaching dinner: they would puff tobacco smoke in the direction of the owl and tempt it by saying 'do you wish to eat tomorrow? Tomorrow I shall catch five or ten deer.' This, they believed, would ensure them of a successful hunt on the morrow. This old Indian belief possibly led to another widely-held hunting superstition in America, particularly heeded when raccoon or opossum hunting, that an owl hoot foretold either good or bad fortune, according to whether it was heard on the right or left hand side: three hoots on the left sent any hunter home in despair. The direction you were facing at the time was obviously crucial and this belief was perhaps related to the one held in parts of North Carolina, that if an owl hooted on the west side of the mountain, it denoted good weather (and good hunting?), but if on the east, bad weather (and hence presumably less inclination to go out and get cold and wet, so that hunting could be honourably postponed).

There is, however, a certain amount of agreement on some issues. To take weather as an example, one of the earliest mentions of the owl's meteorological abilities comes from the Greek Theophrastus, who wrote that 'an owl hooting quietly in a storm indicates fair weather; and also when it hoots quietly by night in winter' (*On weather signs*, c. 300 BC) – though the sceptic could argue that if you could hear a quiet hoot, the storm was obviously passing! These two beliefs persisted: in Britanny, an owl hooting in the evening meant fine weather for the next day. In some other regions of France, a Screech Owl 'singing' during a rain storm meant that fine weather was on the way. In North America, the Pawnee, Omaha and Osage peoples also believed that an owl was a prophet of fair weather: the Osage said that an owl hooting at dawn meant the day would be mild and clear. However, rain storms were

'The owl whose midnight screech disturbs the ghouls.' Grimm Brothers, 19th century.

'The owl is out' – an Athenian proverb meaning: 'we are in luck.'

foretold by owls screeching in parts of Ontario and Newfoundland, whereas in England the same behaviour predicted the approach of a hail storm.

Canny European farmers in Germany, England and parts of France

Archaic owl found on the Acropolis in Athens.

would hang up a dead owl on a barn door as this was said to avert rain and hail storms, thunder and lightning (rather like gargoyles on medieval cathedrals which were said to protect the buildings from evil spirits). But such practices had old antecedents, for Columella, in the first century AD, also mentions that owls were hung up by the Romans to avert storms, and the Ainu of northern Japan used to carve totems representing their divine ancestor, the Eagle Owl, and would nail them to door posts and windows – as a protection – in times of pestilence or famine. In ancient China, too, some two thousand years ago, Han houses had ornamental features, called 'owl corners', which were to act as a protection against fire.

Northerly winds and cold weather have been widely associated with

owls. Both the Chippewas and the Algonquins of North America believed that owls themselves created the northerly winds, and further north the Tetons said the Gray Screech Owl foretold the approach of cold weather. When the night was very cold, this owl cried out, just as if a person's teeth were chattering. When people heard it they would wrap themselves in their thickest robes, and put plenty of wood onto the fires. The Iroquois also went wood-gathering for fires when they heard owls calling, for it meant snow.

In some southern American states, a Little Owl hooting meant cold weather coming. Further north, and in Canada, it was the Snowy Owl, setting out south in search of food and shelter, which heralded the true arrival of winter, although in an old Siberian tale, the Snowy Owls were left behind in the winter when all the other birds migrated south, as a punishment for having tried to deceive them about the existence of a warm place in which to spend the winter months. Thus they tended to stay quite far north, clad in an abundance of white feathers, with their legs 'in such an exuberance of long thick hair-like plumage as to appear as those of a middle-sized dog.' (Alexander Wilson). Two of these owls arrived one year, Wilson tells us, and alighted on the court-house in Cincinnati, Ohio. The inhabitants of the town were a hardened lot, for:

'... a people more disposed to superstition would have deduced some dire or fortunate prognostication from their selecting such a place but the only solicitude was how to get possession of them, which after several vollies was at length affected.'
(Alexander Wilson, *American Ornithology*, 1804–14)

A much sadder fate befell a Horned Owl in a story told by the Grimm brothers. It all happened in a small town in Germany, inhabited by highly superstitious burghers:

Late one night, a Horned Owl from some neighbouring woods ventured into the barn of one of the townsfolk. When day broke, the owl was afraid to leave the barn, for experience had taught it that the people created such an uproar at seeing it, that it was safer to remain hidden until nightfall.

Unfortunately, it was spotted during the morning by a man-servant fetching some straw. Seeing the owl sitting high up on the rafters, he fled to his master, claiming that some monster, the likes of which he had never before seen, was hiding in his barn.

The master was made of sterner stuff, and went to see for himself. But, when on entering the barn he spied two large round eyes staring at him out of the gloom, he lost his nerve, and ran to his neighbours for help. Soon the whole town had heard of this ferocious monster and,

Opposite. Horse-brass. Worn particularly by 'heavy horses' on festive occasions, horse-brasses owe their origins to the amulets once worn by domestic animals to ward off the evil eye.

Sweet Suffolk owl, so trimly dight,
With feathers like a lady bright,
Thou singest alone, sitting at night,
Te whit, te whoo, te whit, te whit.
Thy note, that forth so freely rolls
With shrill command the mouse controls,
And sings a dirge for dying souls,
Te whit, te whoo, te whit, te whit.
(Thomas Vantor, 1619)

94

armed with pitchforks, brooms, sticks and stones, they all made their way to the barn. Then, the most courageous of them pushed open the door and rushed in, but soon retreated, speechless with fear. Some more intrepid men ventured in, but without luck. Then a strong and brave fighting man said he would try. Dressed in armour, clutching his sword and a ladder, he went into the barn, all the time invoking the help of St George who had slain the dragon. Up the ladder he went, until he came face to face with the owl, which by now was so disturbed and frightened that it began to fly around the barn, calling out in fear.

Hearing the commotion inside, the townspeople decided there was only one way to rid themselves of this monster. First they had a collection among themselves for the man who owned the barn, and then they set light to the hay and straw in the barn, pushed the great doors closed, and soon the whole building was ablaze, with the poor owl inside.

People disposed to superstition and even some who claim they are not, widely assume that the owl's arrival does in fact have some deep significance. For instance, in many widely scattered parts of the world, owls are associated with women in one way or another. Mention has already been made of their association with some Aborigine women in Australia. In parts of ancient China, an owl was said to be the soul of a woman who had died in childbirth. In old Babylon, on the other hand, owls were associated with amulets to protect women during labour. In England women dreaded the hoot of an owl at the birth of a child, for it signified that the child would have an unhappy life: 'The owl shrieked at thy birth, an evil sign', Shakespeare's future Richard III is told, but an

Fifteenth-century ceiling tiles from Valencia, Spain.

Contemporary Polish *pisanka*
(decorated Easter egg) by Agnieszka
Sikorska. The egg shell is boiled in a
natural dye (onion skins) and the
design is produced by etching the shell
with a fine point. The egg is an ancient
symbol of life, often associated with
creation myths. According to a Polish
legend, the Virgin Mary painted eggs to
please the Infant Jesus. Since then, eggs
are decorated and given to friends and
relatives at Easter time to celebrate the
Resurrection of Christ.

owl hoot in France at the birth of a child was not quite so dire, for it merely foretold the birth of a daughter.

The owl that entered the lying-in room where the future Emperor Nintoku of Japan (fourth century AD) was born, was regarded as a good omen for the future. This was in complete contrast to current beliefs held about the owl. Normally, in Japan, the owl was held in suspicion and regarded as the symbol of filial ingratitude, for it was said that the owl would eat even its own mother.

Contemporary German sculpture by Eva Lindner-Fritz. The work stands in the gardens of the castle in Karlsruhe.

E.A. Armstrong, in his study on 'night's black agents', as he called them, speculates on whether this connection between owls and women might have originated with the owl's nightly, and hence 'lunar' activities, the lunar phases of the month, and women's monthly cycle (*Folklore of Birds*, 1958). There are further superstitions connected with this notion. In Lorraine, in eastern France, women of thirty or forty who were not yet married would go out into the forests and call to the owl, though how this conjured up a husband, we do not know. In south Wales it was thought that an owl hooting near a house meant that a young girl was about to lose her virginity — fascinating speculation for the local villagers! Strangely, in distant Illinois, exactly the opposite belief was held: if a woman happened to be sitting under a tree where an owl hooted, she would never marry. This belief came full circle in parts of Germany, where the owl was said to be the ghost of a nun, and in Chateaubriand, in France, there was a similar belief which stated that the owl was the soul of an unmarried woman, and the local peasants could even identify which one.

There is, however, one truly worldwide belief, held by so many different peoples, and at so many different times — in North and South America, throughout most of Europe, in Africa and many countries of Asia — that it surely requires some explanation: namely, that hearing or seeing an owl is an omen of death or some other disaster.

> The screech owl, with ill-boding cry
> Portends strange things, old women say ...
> (Lady Mary Wortley Montagu, *The Politicians*,
> 18th century)

It is not always clear whether the owl itself brings the death, or whether it merely announces its imminent arrival. As mentioned earlier, birds — because of their ability to fly — have often symbolised souls and spirits, and the owl, because of its night-time excursions, is linked with nightly spirits. Death and darkness are closely associated in our minds, and so the owl, emerging from the shadows — a ghostly presence, appearing momentarily and then disappearing, uttering its mournful and at times unearthly hoots and screeches — is easily associated with departing souls and ghosts. Owls may in fact be the cause of houses being described as 'haunted'.

By contrast, seeing the owl at an 'unnatural' time, by daylight, equally portends something unpleasant. If an owl was seen on a public building in Rome at midday, it was sure to be foretelling some disaster:

'The scritche owle betokeneth always some heavy news, and is most execrable and accursed in the presaging of public affairs . . . if he be seen either within cities or otherwise abroad in any place, it is not for good, but prognosticates some fearful misfortune.'

(Pliny, *Natural History*, 1st century AD)

However, Pliny assured his readers that this applied only if the owl settled on some public building, and not if it landed on a private dwelling.

Ella Sykes recalls a similar fear in Persia. Remembering her time in the British consulate in Kerman at the beginning of this century, she wrote:

Xaverio Manetti, *Ornithologia Methodice Digesta . . .*, 1767–76. In his caricatures of birds Manetti was probably satirising the mannerisms of contemporary Italian society.

100

'The owls are hunting. Look, over Bethesda gravestones one hoots and swoops and catches a mouse by Hannah Rees, Beloved Wife.' (Dylan Thomas, *Under Milk Wood*, 1954)

Photograph by Colin Turner of a tombstone in Cavendish Church, Suffolk.

'Owls are considered to bring disaster to a house. When living in Kerman, in southeast Persia, I was anxious to have as a pet a lovely little owl. Our servants, however, went in a body to the Persian Secretary, and begged him to ask me not to do so, as the bird would be sure to bring evil to the consulate.'

(Ella Sykes, *Journal of Folklore*, 1901)

A similar event occurred some years earlier in what was then British Senegambia. An owl, Nero, was installed in Government House, whereupon as a visitor recalled:

'... all the servants came in a body to remonstrate, asserting he was a *gumbi* owl, a fetish, and would destroy and kill whatever object he looked on. The chief groom insisted that every cock and hen would go dead. Strangely enough, an epidemic broke out, and carried off from fifty to sixty head of fowl ...'

(Source unknown)

Indeed, in parts of West Africa even today the owl is still considered 'ju-ju' and just looking at it is said to bring bad luck. A European in India recently encountered a similar fear. He was wandering through a temple when a young owl fell out of its nest; he picked it up to put it into the safety of a nearby hedge, but was told by Indian onlookers not to touch it for it was sure to bring him bad luck.

Back in England, Charles Waterton's Yorkshire housekeeper also 'knew full well what sorrow [the owl] brought into houses when she was a young woman ... it was a well-known fact that if any person were sick in the neighbourhood, it would be for ever looking in at the window, and holding a conversation outside with somebody, they did not know with whom. The gamekeeper agreed with her in everything she said on this important matter.' (Charles Waterton, *Essays on Natural History*, 1838).

Disaster also arrived in the shape of an owl in ancient Egypt and later in Ethiopia. When the king had no further use for a minister, he would not request his resignation, but would send him instead the image of an owl. And Flavius Josephus – the ancient Jewish historian – tells us how Herod Agrippa knew the hour of his death had come when an owl appeared. In distant Mexico, and in Morocco, on the other hand, the

Opposite. Little Owl by Albrecht Dürer, 1508.

Page 104. Photograph by Eric Hosking of an immature Spotted Eagle Owl.

102

103

'the wretched hornid owle of helle'
(15th century).

106

Page 105. Tawny Owls by Eric Ennion.

Page 105. Tawny Owls by Eric Ennion.

Opposite. Owl from Hell by Stach, a contemporary Polish painter, 1983. This work is an allegory of the troubled times the artist lives in.

hoot of an owl was merely a bad omen for any traveller about to set out on a journey.

To prevent the occurrence of whatever the owl had in store for you there were various means of driving the omen – or the owl – away. If you lived in Jamaica you cried out 'salt and pepper for your mammy'; in a strangely similar belief, in the Bordeaux region of France, farmers threw salt into the fire. Water could be equally effective: an old Jewish belief was that the owl hoot caused the death of young children in particular, but water poured onto the courtyard of the house where it had been heard would avert the danger. Presumably giving up something that was scarce and therefore valuable – such as water in the desert – appeased the evil spirits.

Strangely, an English child held no such fears about the owl, for he would rhythmically recite:

> Of all the gay birds that e're I did see,
> The owl is the fairest by far to me,
> For all day long it sits on a tree,
> And when night comes away flies he.

And yet it was the owl who, in another nursery rhyme, dug the grave and buried poor cock-robin when he had been cruelly shot down by the sparrow.

Pen drawing by J.C. Parafamunt.

Clay bottle with spout, Ecuador, 1550–500 BC.

The simplest way, of course, of avoiding the calamities foretold by the owl was to pretend you had not heard it – which is what people in parts of Mexico used to do: they blocked their ears. But if you could not help hearing it, the *Rig Veda*, one of the holy books of India, urged the pious to send up prayers to the god of death, and so prevent someone from dying. The seventeenth-century friar, Francesco Guazzo, however, took a decidedly hysterical view, and stated in his *Compendium Maleficarium* that any sighting of owls, along with that of goats and women, was a manifestation of evil!

Yet superstitions and beliefs die hard. Two hundred years later, W.H. Hudson, travelling through southern England, encountered an old man who, when told he had been listening to owls, fixed him with a beady eye:

'"Owls, listening to the owls!" he exclaimed, staring at me. After a while, he added, "We have been having too much of the owls at

Saintbury." Had I heard, he asked, about the young woman who had dropped down dead a week or two ago, after hearing an owl hooting near her cottage in the day time? Well, the owl had been hooting again in the same tree, and no-one knew who it was for and what to expect next. The village was in an excited state about it, and all the children had gathered near the tree and thrown stones into it, but the owl had stubbornly refused to come out.'

(W.H. Hudson, *Birds and Men*, 1901)

Woodcut by Eric Fitch Daglish from
The Birds of E. Fitch Daglish (1925).

People in other parts of the world tried somewhat subtler means of getting rid of the ominous owl. The Takelma Indians of south-west Oregon tried talking to it, in an attempt to have the death 'removed' from their family. They greeted the owl with the following incantation: 'Did you come to give me news? Look up there to the north. See who has been killed. Far away there are many people. Did you see them there? Have many people died there? Is this the news you have come to give me?'

Trying to distract the owl from its purpose was a common practice. In Louisiana, certain Blacks believed that to avoid the bad luck associated with the owl, you had to stick a knife into a piece of wood, or squeeze your wrist – thus killing the owl by strangulation. In coastal regions of Alabama you turned your pockets inside out, and spilt sand into the owl's eyes. In a Zuni Indian legend, it is the other birds who threw sand into the owl's eyes – which is yet another reason why the owl stays 'indoors' during the daytime.

It is possible that the fear of the owl originated in the old homelands of the Blacks, for some peoples of Nigeria, for instance, also dreaded the owl, and would not mention it by name. Instead they would identify it by saying 'the bird that makes you afraid'. Even in Sweden people were loathe to mention the owl by name, for it was a bird of witchery.

'Omens are always true', stated the sixteenth-century dramatist, Calderón, and this certainly seems to have been accepted by the Duke of Dorset, Max Beerbohm's hero. While in pursuit of the delightful Zuleika Dobson, he receives the following telegram from Jellings:

'Deeply regret inform your Grace
last night two black owls came and perched on battlements
remained there through night hooting
at dawn flew away none knows whither
awaiting instructions.'

To which the unfortunate Duke had no option but to reply:

'Prepare vault for funeral Monday.'

... and drowned himself. (Max Beerbohm, *Zuleika Dobson*, 1911).

Having the odds thus stacked against you must have been difficult. For example, a Zuni Indian playing the game of 'hidden ball' and hearing an owl hoot, automatically knew he had lost ... which presumably affected his play thereafter; almost a self-fulfilling prophecy, one might say. 'The owl' was also the name given to the worst throw in the old Chinese game known as *shu-p'u wu-mu*, played with five wooden

110

The large white owl that with eye is blind
That hath sate for years in the old tree hollow
Is carried away in a gust of wind.
(Elizabeth Browning, *Isobel's Child*, 19th century)

Barn Owl by R.G. Greenhalf.

black and white counters. Five black was the best throw, and two white and three black the worst.

The owl itself was the centre-piece of a 'sport', if that is the correct word, at the so-called Hungerford revels, which took place at the town of that name in Wiltshire, southern England. At the revels held in 1820 this 'very laughable but certainly very cruel amusement' was played in the following manner:

'They tie a poor unfortunate owl in an upright position to the back of a still more unfortunate duck, and then turn them loose. The owl, presuming that his inconvenient captivity is the work of the duck, very unceremoniously commences an attack on the head of the latter, who naturally takes to its own means of defence, the water: the duck dives with the owl on its back; as soon as he rises, the astonished owl opens wide his eyes, turns about his head in a very solemn manner, and suddenly recommences his attack on the oppressed duck, who dives as before. The poor animals generally destroy each other unless some humane person rescues them ... Like all other Wiltshire amusements, the Hungerford revels always close with good humour and conviviality ...'

(Letter to the editor of the *Every-Day Book*, 1826)

Athenian silver tetradrachm, classical style, 2nd half of 5th century BC.

Athenian silver tetradrachm, hellenistic style, 2nd century BC.

After such a litany of woes and evil, it is quite a relief to find that some people did actually quite like the owl. In parts of Asia Minor, women seeing an owl would exclaim: 'Good news for us, good messages from you'; and in parts of northern England it was considered good luck to see a White Owl in particular.

The Athenians had an especially soft spot for the Little Owl, Athene's bird. This owl was protected and inhabited the Acropolis in such numbers that the phrase 'taking owls to Athens' had the same connotation as the later English one of 'carrying coals to Newcastle'. The Little Owl not only gave the armies of Athens great confidence, but also kept a watchful eye on Athenian trade and commerce from the reverse side of their coins.

SILLY OWL ~ WISE OWL?

The ambivalence of our feelings about owls is well expressed in a local saying from the Abruzzi in southern Italy: 'Lucky where it settles; woe where it looks'. Even Henry Thoreau, the nineteenth-century American philosopher-naturalist, seemed slightly ambiguous, calling them 'wise midnight hags'. Nor is it entirely clear what Joseph Dennie, the late eighteenth-century Bostonian essayist, had in mind when he called Harvard University a 'roost of owls', but since he also called it a 'sink of vice' and a 'temple of dullness' the description was probably derogatory.

In India too, the owl is synonymous with stupidity and pomposity. *Ullu ki tarah* – in the manner of an owl: acting foolishly; *ullu banana* – to make a fool of someone – are commonly used expressions.

Why man, in the western tradition at least, should have regarded the owl as a symbol of wisdom is not always clear: perhaps it is the owl's almost human appearance – its 'face' – which prompted our vanity to endow this bird with qualities which we ourselves seek; or maybe it is the motionless owl, sitting in a tree, gazing out at the world, in what appears to us a contemplative, philosophical way. But John Gower, the fourteenth-century English poet, was unimpressed by the owl's solemn postures and its apparently motionless existence, and described it as a symbol of sloth, one of the Seven Deadly Sins.

King Milinda, in the old Buddhist text, was advised by the wise Nagasena to emulate the owl:

'Venerable Nagasena, those two qualities of the owl you say [the king] should have, which are they?

Just, o King, as the owl, being at enmity with the crows, goes at night where the flocks of crows are and kills numbers of them; just so, o King, should the strenuous Bhikshu, earnest in effort, be at enmity with ignorance; seated alone and in secret, he should crush it out of existence, cut it off at the root. This, o King, is the first quality of the owl he ought to have.

And again, o King, as the owl is a solitary bird, just so, o King, should the strenuous Bhikshu, earnest in effort, be devoted to solitude, take delight in solitude. This, o King, is the second quality of the owl he should have.'

(*Sacred Books of the East: The Questions of King Milinda*, 1894)

Opposite. Pigmy Owl by Graham Rust. Detail from *The Temptation*, a mural at Ragley Hall, Warwickshire, 1969–83.

114

Apart from being considered wise, the owl was allegedly helpful in times of trouble and warfare. This was certainly what the Fox Indians believed: they regarded owls as their protectors or *manitous:* 'we often meet and converse; they understand us and we understand them.'

And yesterday the bird of night did sit
Even at noonday, upon the market place,
Hooting and shrieking.
(William Shakespeare, *Julius Caesar*)

Roman hand-moulded oil lamp, probably from Corfu, c.40–80 AD.

To prove their point, they carried an owl into war with them, for it was able to cross deep rivers and heal the wounded. The Kiowa Indians were also convinced that the owl once warned them of the approach of their sworn enemies, the Apaches. And on at least two occasions, in places far apart in both time and geography, an owl is said to have saved two monarchs who were being pursued by enemies. King Charles II of England hid in a tree, the famous oak at Boscobel; an owl, perched on the tree as the Roundheads searched for Charles, convinced them that no one could be hiding in such a doomed place. Sir John Mandeville, who in the fourteenth century travelled to the court of Genghis Khan in central Asia, also recounted how the Great Khan was saved by an owl: as he and his small army were fleeing from their enemies, his horse was killed, and he hid under a bush; an owl, alighting upon it, convinced his pursuers that nobody would seek refuge where the dreaded owl perched.

One of the most helpful – though possibly calculating – owls in literature must surely be the sage, if sometimes pompous, owl who, in Washington Irving's *Legend of Prince Ahmed* (1832), helped that lovelorn hero to find his beautiful princess and obtain her hand. At first the owl was reluctant to accompany the Prince in his search: 'Go to, am I a bird to engage in a love affair. I, whose time is devoted to meditation and the moon.' But realising that one day the Prince would be King, and that he would need a Minister, the owl soon changed his mind. From then on, the owl helped the Prince on several important occasions: he not only guided him to Toledo – for the Prince had never before ventured beyond the walls of the Generalife palace – but he also found for him a magical suit of armour and a fine Arab steed with whose aid the Prince became the hero of the tournament arranged for the suitors competing for the Princess's hand. At the same time the Prince also captured the Princess's heart. However, his suit of armour lost its magic at midday and he had to abandon the tournament in a hurry, leaving the Princess in a deep melancholy. Once again the owl came to the rescue. Through a society of owls who met regularly in the Treasury belonging to the Princess's father, he discovered the existence there of a magic carpet. As soon as the Prince, disguised as a peasant, had cured the Princess of her melancholy (in response to her father's pleas), he asked for the carpet as his reward, and, laying it at her feet, he carried her away on it . . . to happiness. And when the Prince finally became King, the owl naturally became his chief Minister.

The author of the 'Owl' entry in the *Encyclopaedia Britannica*, however, had apparently not heard of the owl's exploits, or else remained highly sceptical:

'Owl ... those who know the grotesque actions and ludicrous expressions of this veritable buffoon of birds can never cease to wonder at its having been seriously selected as the symbol of learning, and can hardly divest themselves of a suspicion that the choice must have been made in the spirit of sarcasm.'

(*Encyclopaedia Britannica*, Eleventh Edition)

Harsh though this judgement may be, the owl often does seem to have taken itself rather too seriously. Indeed, Washington Irving's owl would have been highly insulted at the insinuation of stupidity, for he claimed:

Silver ink-stand, 19th century.

'... my nights are taken up in study and research, and my days in ruminating in my cell upon all that I have learnt ...'

Such night-time reading worried Edmund Dulac, although his owl had no claims to erudition:

O was an obstinate owl
  Who could have been quite a nice fowl;
    But she spoilt her eye sight
Reading novels at night.
Now she ogles at you with a scowl.
    (Edmund Dulac, *Lyrics Pathetic and Humorous*,
    1908)

Nevertheless, years of study did not always enable the owl to distinguish between wisdom and conceit, as Aesop's moral tale of the fifth century BC tells us:

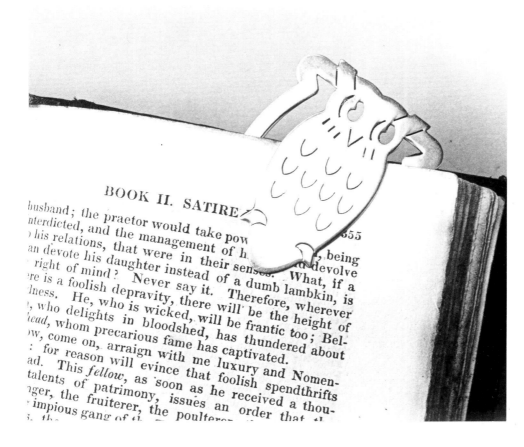

BOOK II. SATIRE

husband; the praetor would take pow... being
interdicted, and the management of h... devolve
his relations, that were in their senses. What, if a
an devote his daughter instead of a dumb lambkin, is
right of mind? Never say it. Therefore, wherever
re is a foolish depravity, there will be the height of
lness. He, who is wicked, will be frantic too; Bel-
, who delights in bloodshed, has thundered about
ead, whom precarious fame has captivated.
w, come on, arraign with me luxury and Nomen-
: for reason will evince that foolish spendthrifts
ad. This *fellow*, as soon as he received a thou-
talents of patrimony, issues an order that
ger, the fruiterer, the poulter...
impious gang of th...

Contemporary silver bookmark.

120

'A formal, solemn owl had for many years made its home in the ruins of an old monastery, and had pored so often over mouldy manuscripts, the stupid relics of a monkish library, that he grew infected with the pride and pedantry of the place and, mistaking gravity for wisdom, would sit whole days with his eyes half shut, fancying himself profoundly learned. It happened, as he sat one evening half buried in meditation and half asleep, that a nightingale, unluckily perching near him, began her melodious lays. He started from his reverie and with a horrid screech interrupted her song. "Begone", he cried, "thou impertinent minstrel, nor distract with noisy dissonance my sublime contemplations. And know, vain songster, that harmony consists in truth alone, which is gained by laborious study, and not in languishing notes, fit only to soothe the ear of a love-sick maid." "Conceited pedant", returned the nightingale, "whose wisdom lies only in feathers that muffle up thy unmeaning face; music is a natural and rational entertainment, and though not adapted to the ears of an owl, has ever been relished by all who are possessed of true taste and elegance".'

The nightingale was lucky, for according to a belief held by some Blacks in Louisiana, the penalty to be paid for mocking an owl was to have your house burnt down. They also believed, in any case, that owls were 'old people' and should never be mocked.

The rat who tried to trick the owl was less lucky, according to a Zuni Indian tale: Owl was sitting asleep, on a pile of stones, while nearby Ground Rat was busy storing corn for the winter. He would dig holes in the ground, and each time one had been filled, would stop work, and sing a little song to himself. This, of course, kept Owl awake. So he flew down, caught Rat by the neck, and told him to stop disturbing him. 'Let me go', squealed Rat, 'I have some beads here, I'll give them to you.' So Owl let Rat go, and Rat scurried to his home, laughing. 'I tricked you, I don't have any beads.' Owl returned to his pile of stones, and pretended to sleep; but as soon as Rat came out once again, Owl flew down, caught him, and ate him!

Above. French bronze figurine by François Pompon, 19th century.

The owl does not seem to have had many friends in the bird and animal kingdoms. But it is, so to speak, a 'chicken and egg' situation: did the

121

other creatures dislike him for his scorn and treachery, and hence did he deserve what he got; or should we feel sorry for a misunderstood bird, constantly disturbed and harassed by the day-birds, who do not understand a creature different from themselves?

A Burmese tale lays the blame squarely on the owl: the cuckoo, the master of the art of healing, refused to help the owl who was in pain, saying that the owl was a treacherous bird and would not pay his fees once he was cured. However, on the pleas of the crow, the owl's friend, he did look at him and told the owl to sit in a pool of water until the pain had gone. And, as the cuckoo predicted, the pain disappeared, but the owl refused to pay, saying the water, not the cuckoo, had cured him. The cuckoo complained to the crow. They both went in search of the owl, but he had flown. The judge in the court said that the crow would have to pay; but since he was a pauper, he was ordered instead to look after the cuckoo's eggs. Angry, the crow went in search of the owl . . . to kill him. The owl, afraid, went into a hole in a tree, and dared to come out only at night. But the crow still searches for the owl, while the owl for ever cowers by day in his hole.

This deep hatred that crows and owls have for one another recurs in tales from countries as far apart as Japan and Spain, and Aristotle also mentions it:

Above. Little Hawk Owl from *A Natural History of Uncommon Birds* by George Edwards, 1743–51. This drawing was used as a model for the porcelain figure shown on the right.

Opposite. Little Hawk Owl, Chelsea porcelain, 18th century. This piece once belonged to Lady Charlotte Schreiber – a late nineteenth-century art lover. It formed part of the porcelain collection she referred to as her 'Chelsea aviary.'

122

124

Opposite. Greek terracotta scent bottle, c.650–625 BC.

'In the winter of 1185, the owls ... in many parts [of the country] produced their young at Christmas-time. Perhaps this foretold some new and unexpected evil'. (Geraldus Cambriensis, *History and Topography of Ireland*, first read in 1188).

'The crow and owl are enemies; for at midday the crow, taking advantage of the dim sight of the owl, secretly seizes and devours its eggs, and the owl eats those of the crow during the night; and one of these is master during the day, the other during the night.'
(Aristotle, *History of Animals*, 4th century BC)

Here Aristotle also touches on the other – and most likely – cause of the hatred between the crow and the owl: a battle over who should be king and master. One of the world's oldest collection of tales, from which

فلما راى ما لقى اهتم وحزن ثم فكر فى امنٍ وعاد عظماً اصحابه

فاستشارهم وذكر لهم الذى اصابه وما يتخوف من حيلتهم ه

مثلا واشد منها عليهم وكان من خمس غرابٍ ذوى رأى ٍ وتجرب

وعلم بالامور ونظرٍ ومكر ٍ وخداعٍ وحيل فخاطبهن وسأطرَحَ ن

رأيهم فيما اصابنهم وقال لاصغرهم ماذا تشير به نانَه

Owls and crows fighting, from a fourteenth-century Syrian manuscript of the Mamluk period, illustrating the fables of *Kalila and Dimna* (the names of the two jackals who play a central role in the stories). The fables were intended as a guide to the conduct of princes.

Late Victorian diamond *tremblant* brooch.

Silent gliding
Nightly questor,
Unruffled, perplexing
Winged cat.
(Anon)

Royal Doulton vase painted by Harry Allan, early 20th century. Allan's bird paintings were considered among the finest in the porcelain industry of the time.

many subsequent ones have been adapted, the *Panchatantra*, compiled in India from Buddhist sources some time around the fourth century BC, describes the beginnings of this long-lasting duel:

The birds had gathered to consider the choice of a new king. Garuda, their present king, was too occupied in serving holy Vishnu, and the birds felt neglected: 'What use is a king who fails to protect us when we are in danger, or when we have been caught in traps? There must be someone else whom we could elect as our king.' Noticing that the owl looked suitably wise, they said 'Let this owl be our king', and they set about organising his coronation.

At this moment, the crow appeared, and knowing him also to be a wise bird, and in a slight change of heart, the birds said: 'You know we have no real king, and we have unanimously decided to annoint the owl as our new king. But give us your opinion, too.' At which the crow laughed maliciously, and said:
'Ugly, cruel, spiteful bird,
All he says is mean and hard;
If you crown the owl your king
No success will come your way.'

(from the *Panchatantra*, c. 4th century BC)

Needless to say, the coronation was abandoned.

In the later Arabian *Tales of Bidpai*, the birds were still pursuing their relentless battle. The crows had built their nests in the trees, and the

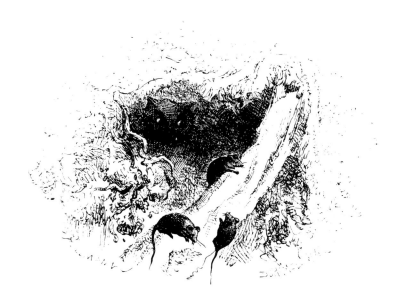

owls in the caves. As the fighting raged, the crows' nests were burnt down by the owls; in revenge, the crows smoked out the caves of the owls (the moral being: never trust your enemy).

The crows were not the owl's only enemy: the eagle, vulture, and raven all took their turns to have disputes with it. In the majority of these tales, the owl is the loser; but in a legend from the Hindu epic, the *Ramayana* (c. 4th–6th century BC), it is the vulture who has to give way: a vulture and an owl who had lived in a particular wood since the beginning of time had a dispute over who owned a certain cave, each of them claiming it by ancient right. They decided to bring the matter before Rama, for his decision. The vulture said:

'The cave has been my home since men, newly created, inhabited the earth.' The owl said: 'It has been my home since the earth was decorated with trees.' Rama decided that the cave belonged to the owl, as trees and plants were created before mankind emerged from the marrow of two demons.

The bigger birds may have had their disputes – based on their individual attempts to retain superiority over their potential rivals – but certainly many small birds came seeking the owl's advice, even though in many instances they ignored it. As we have seen, humans have also sometimes turned to owls for help and protection. There is a Pawnee Indian creation myth which tells how, when all living things lived under the ground in confusion, and decided they needed to explore the land above, it was the owl who led them through the impenetrable forests and showed them the way out.

However, it is perhaps the Hawaiians, more so than most other peoples, who have shown the greatest affection for the owl, which has been their protector throughout the ages. On various occasions, so it is told, they were saved individually by the intervention of owls: Napaepae of Lahaina, who capsized in the channel of Pailola, had to swim all night, and would have drowned but for the owl which flapped its wings in his face and attracted his attention to land nearby; a warrior in King Kamehameha's army, in the thick of battle, was about to plunge head first over some cliffs when an owl flew up and saved him. And a whole gathering of owls came to the help of Kapoi from Honolulu: he had returned some owl's eggs which he had been planning to eat, and

Royal Doulton silicon-ware oil lamp,
19th century.

the owl, in its gratitude, later saved him from the king's wrath. Kapoi had foolishly built a *heiau* (a temple) and had dedicated it – something the king did not allow. On the day of Kapoi's execution, all the owls from Lanai, Maui, Molokai and the Big Island covered the sky over Honolulu, flew at the king's servants as they seized Kapoi, pecked and scratched them, and in the end defeated them. From this time, the owl came to be venerated as a deity by the Hawaiian people and the places where the owls gathered before the battle all have the word *pueo* (owl) in them; the site of the battle in Waikiki is called Kukaenahiokapueo, which means 'confused sound of owls rising in masses'.

On balance, however, the owl does seem to have been scorned and rejected more frequently than listened to and respected. Oliver Goldsmith, the late eighteenth-century English playwright, explained why he, for example, had nothing but contempt for what he saw as the owl's

Etching from Aesop's *Fables*, 1825.

130

underhand behaviour:

'All owls are nocturnal robbers who, unfitted for taking their prey while
it is light, surprise it at those hours of rest, when the tribes of Nature are
in the least expectation of an enemy.'

(Oliver Goldsmith, *History of the Earth and
Animated Nature*, 1808)

As if to prove the point, La Fontaine's fable tells of the cynical owl who
lived in an old tree and fed on:

> ... swarms of mice, who had no toes;
> But never mice were fat as those,
> For Master Owl, who'd snipped and torn
> Day after day fed them on corn.
> The wise bird reasoned thus: 'I've oft
> Caught and stored Mice within my croft
> Which ran away, and 'scaped my claws;
> One remedy is, I'll cut their paws,
> And eat them slowly when I please.

(La Fontaine, *The Owl and the Mice*, 17th century)

Come, doleful owl, the messenger of woe,
Melancholy's bird, companion of despair,
Sorrow's best friend, and mirth's professed foe,
Thy chief discourses that delight sad care.
O come poor owl, and tell thy woe to me
Which having heard, I'll do the like for thee.
(Robert Jones, 1607)

No doubt aware of the mixed feelings it evokes in other animals and in
people, the owl tends to retreat from the world:

> The owl has learnt the world's deceit
> Its vanity and struggles vain,
> And deems it flattery unmeet

131

A thought from reason to obtain.
Apart from the perfidious throng
In wisdom's contemplative mood
To heaven she gives her whole life long,
And steals to holy solitude.
(Azz' Eddin Elmocadessi, *Flowers and Birds*)

Ornithology of Francis Willoughby, 1675.

The owl's contempt and disdain for its fellow birds – and probably for the world at large – furnished Bernard Saisset, the late thirteenth-century Bishop of Pamiers in south western France, with a metaphor to describe his king, the controversial Philippe le Bel:

'The king is like an owl, the most beautiful of birds, but worth nothing. He is the most handsome of men, but he stares fixedly in silence . . . He is neither man nor beast, he is a statue.'

The king, in turn, had this unruly priest tried and convicted as a heretic and a traitor guilty of inciting rebellion.

But it was the owl's wisdom which, in an old Persian tale, furnished a cautious vizier with a parallel when attempting to give his master, the great King Nushirvan, some good advice: Nushirvan was a keen hunter

Opposite. Prairie Evening – Short-Eared Owl, painting by the contemporary Canadian artist, Robert Bateman.

Scops Aldrov.
The *little Horn Owle.*

Page 134. Detail from *Garden of Delights* by Hieronymous Bosch, late 15th century. In late medieval north European art, the owl was a predatory, nocturnal and sinister creature. In Bosch's paintings it was probably used as a symbolic reference to the depravity and wickedness of man. In the *Garden of Delights* it possibly signified lust, one of the Seven Deadly Sins.

So, when the night falls, and dogs do howl!
We know not always
Who are kings by day,
But the king of the night is the bold, brown owl.
(Barry Cornwall, *The Horned Owl*, 19th century)

134

Page 135. Salt-glazed stoneware vase decorated by Florence Barlow, c. 1890. She belonged to the celebrated Barlow family who worked for the Doulton Lambeth studios.

Opposite. A pub sign in Somerset.

'Men will be drunk as owls.'
(popular saying)

and fighter, to the neglect of his subjects. One day, he spotted two owls hooting in a ruined tower of a village, and he asked his vizier what they were saying. His minister thought a parable would be appropriate, and explained that the two owls were discussing the marriage of their son and daughter to one another. The father of the groom demanded a dowry from the father of the bride, in the form of one hundred ruined villages. 'That', said the bride's father, 'I cannot yet provide, but give me time, for soon our Sultan's behaviour will put me in a position to grant you this request.'

Nushirvan was deeply impressed by this tale, and immediately set about repairing and restoring the ruined villages throughout his kingdom.

In ancient China, by contrast, the owl was regarded as a symbol of cruelty and wickedness, and in the allegorical ballads about tyranny and oppression sung across the country, the owl represented the ruthlessness of politicians, destroying innocent lives.

Many centuries later, the owl also served as an unattractive model for the late eighteenth-century Italian writer Giambattista Casti. In his satirical work, *Animali Parlanti*, that deals with the social conflicts arising out of the French Revolution, he portrayed the owls as the

Car radiator mascot by René Lalique, c.1928. Rarest of the Lalique mascots as it was considered ugly, there are only two known examples.

137

insidious ministers of the all-powerful being, the Cuckoo. They kept the other birds and animals in ignorance and subjection, to control them better in the interests of their despotic masters, the eagles and lions. The owls also kept close guard over their own lands, not permitting the other birds and animals to feed on them even after natural disasters (which, naturally, never affected the owls' lands) had devastated the other beasts' fields, leaving them hungry and homeless.

Further proof of the owl's malign character is to be found in an old legend from northern France. A monk in the abbey of St Jacut was condemned, for murder, to be incarcerated for life and to be perpetually tortured and tormented. His gaolers turned out to be owls, who pulled out his hair and his beard to make their nests.

Perhaps Edward Lear had a point after all when he wrote:

There was an old man with a beard
Who said 'It is just as I feared,
Two owls and a hen
Four larks and a wren
Have all built their nests in my beard.'
(Edward Lear, *Nonsense Botany and Nonsense Alphabets*, 1889)

Parables, fables and moral tales serve mankind as useful guidelines for

the sort of behaviour we expect of one another; they pinpoint failings and foibles, virtues and ideals. The owl appears in a great many of them as a figure of fun, a treacherous bird, a source of wisdom, and our century is now adding to the collection.

138

Early nineteenth-century English painted and gilt brass wall candle-holder.

A gold-mounted nephrite bell-push, signed by Michael Perchin, one of the best-known goldsmiths in Carl Fabergé's workshop in St Petersburg.

Let us end on a cautionary tale based around this most fascinating fowl – the owl.

Still as the flight of an owl.
(Nineteenth-century American proverb)

THE OWL WHO WAS GOD

'Once upon a starless midnight there was an owl who sat on the branch of an oak tree. Two ground moles tried to slip quietly by, unnoticed. "You!" said the owl. "Who?" they quavered, in fear and astonishment, for they could not believe it was possible for anyone to see them in that thick darkness. "You two!" said the owl. The moles hurried away and told the other creatures of the field and forest that the owl was the greatest and wisest of all animals because he could see in the dark and because he could answer any question. "I'll see about that," said a secretary bird, and he called on the owl one night when it was again very dark. "How many claws am I holding up?" said the secretary bird. "Two", said the owl, and that was right. "Can you give me another expression for 'That is to say' or 'namely'?" asked the secretary bird. "To wit", said the owl. "Why does a lover call on his love?" asked the secretary bird. "To woo", said the owl.

The secretary bird hastened back to the other creatures and reported that the owl was indeed the greatest and wisest animal in the world because he could see in the dark and because he could answer any question. "Can he see in the daytime, too?" asked a red fox. "Yes," echoed a dormouse and a French poodle. "Can he see in the daytime, too?" All the other creatures laughed loudly at this silly question, and they set upon the red fox and his friends and drove them out of the region. Then they sent a messenger to the owl and asked him to be their leader.

When the owl appeared among the animals it was high noon and the sun was shining brightly. He walked very slowly, which gave him an appearance of great dignity, and he peered about him with large, staring eyes, which gave him an air of tremendous importance. "He's God!" screamed a Plymouth Rock hen. And the others took up the cry "He's God!" So they followed him wherever he went and when he began to bump into things they began to bump into things, too. Finally he came to a concrete highway and he started up the middle of it and all the other creatures followed him. Presently a hawk, who was acting as outrider, observed a truck coming toward them at fifty miles an hour, and he reported to the secretary bird and the secretary bird reported to the owl. "There's danger ahead," said the secretary bird. "To wit?" said the owl. The secretary bird told him. "Aren't you afraid?" he asked. "Who?" said the owl calmly, for he could not see the truck. "He's God!" cried all the creatures again, and they were still crying "He's God!" when the truck hit them and ran them down. Some of the animals were merely

'The cynic is one who never sees a good quality in man, and never fails to see a bad one. He is the human owl, vigilant in darkness and blind to light, mousing for vermin, and never seeing nobler game.' (H.W. Beecher, *Lectures to Young Men*, 19th century)

Sketch by James Thurber.

injured, but most of them, including the owl, were killed.'

Moral: You can fool too many of the people too much of the time.
(James Thurber, *Fables for our Time*, 1940)

PICTURE ACKNOWLEDGEMENTS
The author and Savitri Books extend their particular thanks
to the following individuals and organisations whose help was
invaluable:
Robert Gillmor
Christopher Burton
Robert Bateman
Peyton Skipwith of the Fine Art Society
The staff at Sotheby's, London
The staff of the Bodleian Library, Oxford
The John Rylands University Library, Manchester
The Victoria and Albert Museum
Mallett and Son (Antiques) Ltd

We have endeavoured to obtain permission from every
copyright owner, although, regretfully, in a few instances, we
were unable to trace the artists concerned.

The following museums, art galleries, art dealers, collectors,
artists and photographers have kindly given us permission to
reproduce works of art and artefacts in their possession:
The Albertina, Vienna: 103
Museum of the American Indian, Heye Foundation, New
    York: 12
Norman Arlott: 33
Winifred Austen estate: 37
Robert Bateman and the Mill Pond Press Inc., Venice, Florida:
    133
Bodleian Library, Oxford: Ms. Bodley Rolls 19: 10b; Ms.
    Douce 331, fol. 103: 21; Ms. Hatton 10, fol. 43: 32; Ms.
    Bodley 602, fol. 64v.: 63b: Ms. Laud. Lat. 84, fol. 193r.:
    68: Ms. Autog. G.3, fol. 55v.: 79; Ms. Poc. 400, fol. 94r.:
    125
Museum Boymans-van Beuningen, Rotterdam: 77
The Trustees of The British Museum, London: 116
Burrell Collection, Art Gallery and Museum, Glasgow: 44a,
    56

The Burton family: 61
John Busby: 7
Marianne Calmann: 41 (photographer: Salim Hafejee)
The trustees, The Cecil Higgins Art Gallery, Bedford: 19, 47
Christies, London: 66b, 121, 138
Christies Colour Library, London: half title page, 85
Bruce Coleman Ltd: jacket and frontispiece picture
Barry Driscoll: 84
Field Museum of Natural History, Chicago: 69
Fine Art Society, London: 83
Museum of Fine Arts, Boston: 87
M. Desmond Fitzgerald: 6a, 9, 10a, 13, 15, 16, 27, 48, 70, 73
    (photographer: Colin Turner), 86, 97, 106, 107, 111, 120
Gallerie Moderne, London: 137 (photographer: Andrew
    Stewart)
William Geldart: 82
Robert Gillmor: 52, 53, 57, 105 (in association with Hugh
    Ennion)
Tim Greenwood: 35
Eric Hosking: 104
Angus James: 24
John Rylands University Library, Manchester: Ryl. Latin Ms.
    16, fol. 203r.: 6b: Ryl. Latin Ms. 8, fol. 15r.: 39
Hugh Jones: 58b, 95
Eva Lindner-Fritz: 98
The Council of the Linnean Society of London: 43
Mallett and Son (Antiques) Ltd, London: 26, 55, 93, 118, 139
Mansell Collection, London: 14, 92
Glenis McSwinney: 31
Musées Nationaux, Paris: 124
Phillips, London: 44b, 89, 126, 127b
John Piper: 60
Portal Gallery, London: 59
Prado, Madrid: 134
David Pratt: 36, 143
Punch: 28
Royal Doulton: 126, 129, 135
Royal Society for the Protection of Birds: 54, 67, 132
Graham Rust: 74, 115 (photographer: Louise Hertford, The
    Marchioness of Hertford)
The Robert and Lisa Sainsbury Collection, University of East
    Anglia, Norwich: 80, 108
J.C.D. Smith: 49a, 49b
Sotheby's, London: 5, 20, 23, 40, 58a, 63a, 66a, 71, 100,
    113a, 113b, 119, 122b
Ralph Thompson: 30
Mrs Helen Thurber and Hamish Hamilton: 141
Colin Turner: 101
The Board of Trustees of the Victoria and Albert Museum,
    London: 22, 64, 72, 96, 123
Wadworth Brewers and the landlords of 'The Owl': 136
    (photographer: Nigel Cope)

Pen-and-ink drawing by David Pratt.

TEXT ACKNOWLEDGEMENTS
For permission to use the following copyrighted material, we
would like to thank:
Chatto and Windus and the author for 'An Owl at Night' by R.C.
Trevelyan
Fontana Books for the extract from *The Once and
Future King* by T.H. White
J.M. Dent and Sons Ltd for the quote from *Under Milk Wood* by
Dylan Thomas
Gerald Duckworth and Company Ltd for 'Three Nocturns' by
Osbert Sitwell
Granada Books and Curtis Brown for the extract from *My
Family and Other Animals* by Gerald Durrell
Doubleday and Company, Inc. and Faber and Faber Publishers for
the excerpt from 'The Old Trouper' from *archy and mehitabel*
by Don Marquis. Copyright 1927 by Doubleday and
Company, Inc. Reprinted by permission of the publisher
Mrs. Helen Thurber and Hamish Hamilton Ltd for James
Thurber's 'The Owl Who Was God' from *Vintage Thurber*
edited by Helen Thurber. Copyright © 1940 James Thurber.
Copyright © 1968 Helen Thurber. From *Fables for our Time*,
published by Harper and Row.
Excerpt from *Owl* by William Service. Copyright © 1969
William Service. Reprinted by permission of Alfred A. Knopf,
Inc. and of Cassell and Company Limited
Mrs. Eva Reichmann for the extract from *Zuleika Dobson* by
Max Beerbohm
Trinity College, Cambridge, for the extract from *The Golden
Bough* by J.G. Frazer
Faber and Faber Publishers and the author for 'My Grandpa'
from *Meet my Folks* by Ted Hughes

St. Agnes Eve – Ah bitter chill it was!
The owl for all its feathers was a-cold.
(John Keats, *The Eve of St. Agnes*, 19th century)

When day-light ends
Perched on some ruined tower, the owl in vain
Breathes in the ear of night his mournful strain.
(Virgil, *Georgics*)

Back of jacket. The Learned Owl by
Granville (Jean-Ignace-Isidore Gérard)
– the nineteenth-century satirical
cartoonist.